Ed... e
Urban Crisis

'9 (Fie)

p.6319493

Contents

In bringing together the material for this book I have drawn on the papers which were prepared for the two Calouste Gulbenkian conferences on education and the urban crisis, as well as the contributions which other delegates made during our discussions. Each main development in the debate is prefaced by a short summary which appears in italics in the text.

Jill Sullivan, Jane Jessel and Clare Dennehy all kindly helped to prepare the manuscript for publication and I am grateful to them for their assistance.

Chiswick   Frank Field
September 1976

Introductory Essay

The Calouste Gulbenkian Foundation sponsored two conferences around the theme, *Education and the Urban Crisis*, for the following reasons. First, the Foundation thought it important to try and bring together information on the current trends in our inner city areas in order to judge whether British cities were slipping into a disorder similar to that occurring in the USA. Second, if our cities were beginning to follow the American pattern, the Foundation wanted to know what part our educational system could play in reversing this trend. This introduction draws on the conference papers and discussions to introduce the reader to the two main themes explored in this book. The first part attempts to outline the main economic developments in inner city areas in Britain. In doing so we suggest that use of the term 'urban crisis' is but another way of discussing the persistence of poverty in Britain. The second part of the essay then turns to review the extent to which our schools are contributing to, or can be used to counter, inner city poverty. The conclusion pinpoints the action programme detailed in chapter 4 of the book.

Barry Cullingworth has remarked that the term 'urban crisis' reminds him of a passage from George Orwell's book *The Road to Wigan Pier*. A local miner was asked at what time the housing shortage in the area had become severe. To this question he replied: 'Oh, when we were told about it.' Cullingworth wondered if, in fact, the urban crisis wasn't a similar phenomenon. (Janet Brand and Margaret Cox (eds), *The Urban Crisis: Social Problems and Planning*, Royal Town Planning Institute, 1974.) At what point, then, did urban poverty become the urban crisis; and to what extent are the two synonymous? Are the numbers of poor people increasing and is the incidence of poverty most marked in inner urban areas?

Each year Parliament approves a level of income for claimants dependent on supplementary benefits. Many regard this as the official definition of poverty. It certainly provides us with a generally acceptable yardstick for a discussion on the numbers in poverty. Although a number of writers have drawn attention to the limitations of this approach, it is difficult to argue that the use of the supplementary benefit scale rates will over-estimate the numbers of poor. In their study *The Poor and the Poorest*, Brian Abel Smith and Peter Townsend used the official definition of poverty to estimate the numbers of poor in 1953 and 1960. Their estimates were derived from the Family Expenditure Survey which was initiated by the Government in 1953 and which has been carried out each year since 1960. Before the publication of *The Poor and the Poorest* most people believed that the welfare state had been successful in abolishing poverty. The Abel Smith/Townsend study showed that this was far from true, and that between 1953 and 1960 there had been a considerable increase in the numbers of poor people. If we rework some of the data, we can make a comparison with the numbers in poverty in 1973. Whereas Abel Smith and Townsend found 3·4 million living at incomes at or below 110 per cent of the official poverty line in 1960, this number had increased to a little over 6·5 million by 1973. Furthermore, recent evidence shows that these poor people are disproportionately concentrated in inner city areas.

The conclusion of the Inner Area Study in Liverpool is typical of the findings of most research on the inner city. The authors commented: 'Liverpool's inner area today is diverse in its population, complex in its neglect and decay, and contains a wide variety of problems. Any attempt to summarise its distinctive characteristics risks oversimplification. Nevertheless, a particular combination of features distinguishes it from other areas. They are a falling population; an increasing concentration of those who are poor and of low status in society; a predominantly poor housing stock and a neglected environment, subjected to large scale physical change; and a virtual abandonment by economic activity and productive investment. This culminates in a sense of alienation by many of its inhabitants brought about by poverty, lack of power to influence events affecting their homes and lives, and feelings of insecurity about their future.' The authors went on to note however that it would be wrong to see the inner area as a place apart. 'Rather, it is an integral part of society where the worst results of inequality are most in evidence, where those with least power, and least able to help themselves are to be found' (Inner Area Study, Liverpool, *Third Study Review*, DOE, n.d., p. 3).

That we are still dealing with the extremes of poverty and inequality in our society is a point made by the researchers working in Lambeth, an inner area of London. They cite Rowntree's studies of poverty in York. In *Poverty: A Study of Town Life* (1901) and *Poverty and Progress* (1942) Rowntree drew attention to the fact that large sections of the working population became poor during part of their lives, particularly when they were raising a family or when they were too old to earn a living. The Lambeth researchers were interested in finding out whether Rowntree's analysis was still true today in an inner city area. In their conclusion the researchers state: 'The life cycle of poverty clearly revolves as powerfully as in Rowntree's day. The reason is obvious enough. What the two main troughs of poverty have in common is that income is low in relation to dependency, at one stage just because the income is low (usually just a pension or supplementary benefit or both) and at the other because, though there is an earned income, there are additional dependants' (Inner Area Study, Lambeth, *Poverty and Multiple Deprivation*, DOE, n.d., p. 5).

If the findings on level of real income in inner London are representative of other inner city areas, then the poverty of large numbers of inner city dwellers is being aggravated by real cuts in their standard of living. For the analysis on real income undertaken by the GLC shows a deteriorating position for the poorest 25 per cent of households in the inner London area. Whereas the poorest 25 per cent in the Greater London area and in the South East generally suffered a relative decline in their income during the period 1965–71, the poorest 25 per cent in the Inner London area suffered real cuts in income during the same period (GLC, *Population and Employment*, 1973). Moreover, the same study found that whereas the poorest households' earnings had not kept pace with price increases, many households in the inner area of London found it increasingly difficult to find employment. Other research shows these findings to be true of inner cities generally.

The question of unemployment can be looked at both by measuring the unemployment rate amongst those in inner city areas, and comparing it with other areas and regions of the country, and by specifically looking at the loss of employment opportunities within the inner city. In the seven-year period 1966–72, firms in the London area shed 217,400 people, and these redundancies were mainly in the manufacturing sector. Put another way, something like 22 per cent of the total numbers of jobs in manufacturing industry in the London region disappeared within a seven-year period (Graham Lomas, *The Inner City*, London Council of Social Service, 1974, p. 2).

The Inner Area Study in Liverpool noted that some 67,000 un-skilled manual jobs on Merseyside were lost in the 1960s principally from employment in the docks and railways, both traditionally employers of inner area residents (op. cit., p. 13).

It is not surprising, therefore, that the number of unemployed in the inner city region has grown, nor that this unemployment is concentrated amongst the poorest. One analysis looked at three inner city areas and studied the number of enumeration districts in the 1971 census showing more than 15 per cent male unemploy-ment. In Clydeside there were 1,012 districts, in Merseyside 393 and in the GLC 147, of which 104 were in inner London boroughs. (See Des McConaghy's contribution in *The Urban Crisis: Social Problems and Planning*, p. 41.) Another analysis has shown that the unemployment problems in individual London boroughs are as serious as those in designated development areas in what used to be thought of as the depressed areas of Britain (GLC, op. cit.). For example, in East Ham there were thirty-three registered male unemployed claimants for each vacancy. These figures relate to 1973, when the average for Greater London as a whole was three unemployed male claimants for each vacancy.

The poverty and unemployment of inner city areas are partly a result of successive governments' planning policies. As we shall see from the data presented in chapter 1, emphasis was placed on building new industrial areas outside the main cities at the expense of the opportunities in the inner city. Personnel for new firms were selected on the grounds of ability. Room was found for the more highly skilled, but not for the unemployed or fatherless family. As the more able were enticed away from the inner city, the proportion of poor and disadvantaged left behind rose correspondingly. In one Manchester ward over a third of the households are composed of single-parent families (City of Manchester, *Census Information*, n.d., table 24) and as David Eversley points out, in some areas of London over a third of the households are trapped on means-tested benefit.

The conference considered to what extent economic forces would of themselves counter the increasing problem of poverty in the inner city areas. Without exception contributors came to the view that economic developments in the foreseeable future would probably aggravate rather than abate the employment problems of the inner city. In his contribution Peter Hall points out that we expect to see a growth in service employment during the next ten years, though he was careful to emphasise that many of the new opportunities in the service industry will be for low-paid employment. Latest forecasts show, however, that employment in clerical, sales and service trades, which showed such a rapid expansion between 1961 and 1971, will remain 'fairly stable' in the period up to 1981 with, no doubt, consequential effects on unemployment ('A view of occupational employment in 1981', *DE Gazette*, July 1975). If anything therefore the analysis of the employment potential in the new service industries exaggerated the likely gains for the inner city worker.

It is within this framework of growing poverty and unemployment in inner city areas that the conference turned its discussion to education, and specifically to the examination of three themes: what is happening to educational attainment in schools; to what extent are city schools being increasingly characterised by violence; and are schools failing to develop amongst their pupils skills which are in demand in the labour market? There was no support for the view that education by itself could transform the lives and wellbeing of poor children, for that would require a much wider concerted attack on the inequalities of life chances of the poor. In fact, the possibility that the reverse was occurring was considered. It appeared to some participants that schools were contributing to unrest in inner city areas by their failure to equip pupils with the skills necessary to hold down a reasonable job during their working life. And, as if this was not enough, that we were witnessing a serious decline in educational achievements, particularly in inner city schools, and that many of these schools were characterised by violence and disorder.

The debate about declining educational standards concentrated on what was happening to the level of reading ability of school children. Are the schools producing an increasing number of illiterate persons? One of the difficulties in attempting to answer this question is that the meaning of literacy changes over time. This must be borne in mind when reading the contributions in chapter 2. Lord Bullock has noted: 'It is obvious that as society becomes more complex and makes higher demands in awareness and understanding of its members the criteria of literacy will rise' (*A Language for Life*, HMSO, 1975, p. 11). Thus in 1951 UNESCO was able to say that a person is literate 'who can, with understanding, both read and write a short simple statement on his everyday life'. But a decade later the same organisation had modified its view: 'A person is literate when he has acquired the essential knowledge and skills which enable him to engage in all those activities in which literacy is required for effective functioning in his group and community.' Are reading standards not only being maintained in British schools, but rising significantly enough to match the increased demands placed on ordinary citizens in the ordering of their everyday affairs?

Since 1948 there has been a series of surveys which purport to measure the reading ability of school children. (However, Bullock argues that these tests are not an adequate measure of reading ability; they measure, rather, a narrow aspect of silent reading comprehension.) Some researchers have claimed that it is reasonable to conclude from this survey work that for the sixteen years during which the tests have operated there has been an advance of 17 months in the reading ages of 11-year-old school children and an advance of 20–23 months for 15-year-old children. However, these results need to be considered cautiously. The view that these results show a 'remarkable improvement' in the reading ability of school children has not met with universal support. Some researchers have pointed out that the 1948 test scores were naturally depressed as a result of the war and that they consequently present a low baseline which artificially boosts subsequent results. On the other hand the language of the two reading tests which are used has now dated. How many school children come across the word manikin? Moreover, are many 15-year-olds capable of dealing with more difficult items than the test contains but, because of the construction of the text, not able to register higher scores? If so this will have the effect of depressing both the reading scores of the more able pupils and the average score of the whole sample.

Despite the drawbacks of these tests conducted on a national scale over time, they do allow us to measure the 'reading ability' of children according to their social background. Evidence from the EPA studies shows that non-reading is a serious problem for many poor children. Taking the NFER sentence completion test, and a score of 80 to distinguish non-readers or virtual non-readers, EPA studies show non-readers total 19 per cent, 35·8 per cent, 21·7 per cent and 17·7 per cent of pupils in the four EPA study areas. Even more disturbing are the results from other local studies which show that there has been a decline in the overall reading standards of poor children. We draw on one of these surveys to illustrate this trend.

The study of the reading abilities of school children in Aberdeen compared their attainment in 1962 and in 1972. Overall the difference between the 1962 and 1972 averages is small and it 'would be reasonable to conclude therefore that standards are essentially unchanged over the past ten years'. However, when the averages are broken down for each social class the results 'cannot be passed over complacently. Whereas amongst children whose fathers are in professional managerial jobs, the average standard has improved, or at least been maintained, the picture is different for children whose fathers are in semi-skilled jobs. Their average performance, at age 11, is clearly and seriously below the standards of the equivalent social group ten years ago' (John Nisbet *et al.*, Reading standards in Aberdeen, *Research in Education*, 16, 1975, pp. 172–5).

Falling educational standards (measured by an admittedly inadequate gauge) may well help to explain the alleged increase in behavioural problems in many schools. In 1971 ILEA conducted a follow-up study of the reading standards of children born between 1 September 1959 and 2 September 1960. For those children in the survey teachers were asked to rate their pupils' behaviour according to the Rutter behaviour scale. A fifth of the sample obtained abnormal scores, 11 per cent were classified by their teachers as anti-social and 5 per cent as neurotic (although the author of the report is at pains to make out that these are teacher classifications). Boys were more likely than girls to obtain abnormal scores, and approximately a third of the children in each of the abnormal behaviour categories obtained very low scores on the SRB group reading test. Half the children were given the NFER's DE reading comprehension test while the remaining children were given individual tests – the Neal analysis of reading ability.

The results of these two tests showed a strong relationship between reading ability and behaviour. 'Children without behaviour disorders were, on average, ten months ahead of children with anti-social behaviour . . . when tested for reading accuracy and eleven months ahead of them when tested for comprehension. Children with undifferentiated behavioural difficulties . . . were, on average, sixteen months behind non-deviant children in both reading accuracy and comprehension.' As A. Varlaan, the author of the report, notes, it is no new observation to conclude that there is a link between academic failure and abnormality of behaviour. But he goes on to ask the question, which comes first? If reading retardation is the primary cause, then one would expect children with both reading and behavioural difficulties to resemble children with only reading difficulties more closely than children with only behavioural disorders. After carefully analysing the sample, Varlaan writes in the following terms: 'With two exceptions (parental separation and type of school attended) the group of children with both reading and behavioural difficulties resemble more closely the group of children who had only reading difficulties' (A. Varlaan, 'Educational attainment and behaviour at school', *Greater London Intelligence Quarterly*, December 1974, pp. 30–3). The report concluded by observing that, if abnormalities of behaviour in the schools develop as a reaction to educational failure, then our first priority should be not so much with controlling and rectifying unruly behaviour as with the environmental conditions and the effectiveness of the teaching of children during their first years at school, when the foundations of their future educational attainment are laid. This has important implications for the proposals set out in the last section of the book, the emphasis of which is placed on spreading the success achieved by a minority of schools to many others.

While trying to understand the causes of disorder in schools, it is also important to keep the problem within a proper perspective. The National Association of Schoolmasters (NAS) has been prominent in the campaign, drawing public attention to violent and unruly behaviour in schools. In a report published in 1972 the Association maintained that there is a greater concentration of violence in urban than in rural schools. Further, most of this violence occurs in schools in deprived areas, or areas containing large numbers of socially or economically underprivileged people (L. F. Lowenstein, *Violence in Schools*, National Association of Schoolmasters, 1972).

The 1972 report contained the results of a questionnaire sent to 13,500 schools on the NAS school representative mailing list. From the results of the questionnaire the report concluded 'that the amount of violence varied from school to school but that it "is much larger than might have been anticipated from the occasional press reports" ' (ibid., p. 25). It is officially admitted that there is a behavioural problem in schools, although 'the problem is largely confined to certain areas of the country and to particular schools'. The DES report on the first year after ROSLA went on to remark that 'A small number of difficult pupils can create an effect out of all proportion to their numbers, but misbehaviour, especially violent misbehaviour, is not widespread. Although some of it may be due to the resentment of some pupils who find themselves compelled to stay on at school for another year, it would be nonsensical to attribute all the blame for violent behaviour to this.' And the report remarked that there had always been violent pupils but, of course, 'some of them are now in their fifth year' (DES, *Reports on Education*, no. 83, 1975).

That the problems of misbehaviour are still on a fairly small and therefore manageable scale can be seen from the NAS's own survey. Despite the fact that the report paints a picture of violence being a prominent feature of many schools, the survey results show that only 24 secondary schools out of the 1,065 that replied (of the 13,500 circulated) claimed that violence occurred very frequently in their schools, and this contrasted with 443 schools that replied they had no real problems concerning violence and misbehaviour.

Where the conferences thought there was a much more serious failing was in the area of equipping pupils with skills that would enable them to hold a reasonable job in the inner city area. The conferences were aware that this issue raises the fundamental question about whether the purpose of the education system is to ensure a pool of ability which will sustain the economic system or whether it is to ensure the wellbeing of persons in their local community 'by equipping them to gain mastery over key areas of life together'. It is certainly fashionable to take the neo-Marxist view as expressed, for example, in CDP reports. John Bazalgette, in what is an impressive study on school life and work life in the inner city, performs the statutory genuflection to current views by observing: 'The dominant factor influencing what happens to young men and young women from an area such as Hillfields (Coventry) is the need of the structure of industrial employment, as perceived by the schools, rather than the real needs of young people developing towards adulthood.' And quoting the Coventry CDP report he observes, concerning the relationship of Hillfields community to the Coventry labour market, that: 'the needs of those firms both at times of boom and at times of slump call for a pool of semi and unskilled labour which can be taken on and laid off with comparative ease' (John Bazalgette, *School Life and Work Life in the Inner City*, Grubb Institute, 1975).

Yet if anything stands out clearly, both from Bazalgette's own study and from the contributions of the conference, it is that most schools appear to be a million light years from a situation where they gear their education programmes to the needs of the wider labour market. The Schools Council report on *Closer Links between Teachers and Industry and Commerce* drew attention to the fact that many secondary school teachers felt they neither knew nor understood the industrial and commercial environments in which most of their pupils would eventually have to work (Working Paper no. 7, HMSO, 1966); that the main problem for the school leaver is not so much that the schools are slavishly serving the economic needs of the labour market but rather that they fail to develop their students' talents in a way which enables them to choose more secure and better paid employment. Comments by employers that schools are increasingly failing to provide new recruits with adequate literacy standards are now common. There could hardly be a more effective way of describing the mismatch between what schools produce and what the wider economy needs than the report of the working party set up by the National Youth Employment Council. At one point in the report the Council makes the following observation. 'We have heard it said that careers officers find it easy to help pupils from ESN schools because they come out better equipped to face the world and to tackle a job of work than pupils from the lower streams of comprehensive and modern schools' (Department of Employment, *Unqualified, Untrained and Unemployed*, HMSO, 1974, p. 37).

A three-pronged programme of reform emerged from the conference discussions. First, there was the recognition that the basic problem of poverty remained to be tackled. Second, within this attack on poverty, the Foundations had an important part to play in funding an inner city anti-poverty project. Third, education reforms were proposed which were aimed not only at improving what happened *within* schools, but also at significantly reducing the extent to which our present educational system adds to the problems of the inner city.

In this book we have often defined poverty in purely financial terms. This is not because of a lack of recognition that there are other forms of poverty, but rather because it is believed that by solving the problem of financial poverty we will also be tackling many other forms of deprivation. The attack on financial poverty will need to be launched on two fronts. The first is that of low wages, a point made forcibly by John Vaizey (see page 128). This view has also been put in a slightly different way by Tony Atkinson. He argues that low pay is a thread which runs throughout people's working lifetimes and beyond into retirement. 'Low pay must be seen more generally as a disadvantage in the labour market, and as associated with high incidence of job instability and ill health and with the absence of fringe benefits. The low paid worker is more vulnerable to the interruption or loss of earning power, and lacks the resources to meet such needs. Low earnings mean that people cannot save for emergencies or for old age. They cannot get a mortgage and the only way in which they could borrow is through HP or not paying the electricity bill. In these and other ways, low pay plays an important role in the cycle of poverty' (A. B. Atkinson, 'Low pay and the cycle of poverty' in *Low Pay*, ed. Frank Field, Arrow, 1973).

Second, there is also the need to attack the poverty amongst those who are unable to work. 'To prevent interruption or destruction of earning power from leading to Want, it is necessary to improve the present schemes of social insurance in three directions: by extending the scope to cover persons now excluded; by extension of purpose to cover risks now excluded; and by raising the rates of benefit.' Ruth Lister notes in her proposals for a new Beveridge plan that it is a sad indictment of post-war governments that these words written by Beveridge in 1942 are still relevant over thirty years later (Ruth Lister, *Social Security: the Case for Reform*, Child Poverty Action Group, 1975).

Ruth Lister calculated that it would cost many billions of pounds to implement the Beveridge report fully and to extend benefits free of means tests to those groups, such as many single parents, who are at present not covered by the national insurance scheme. This total includes nothing towards the costs of tackling what is described in the book as urban squalor. Delegates at the conference accepted that such a programme was not going to be introduced 'at a stroke'. Rather, an anti-poverty strategy might well take the life of two Parliaments to implement fully. It is against this realisation that Peter Brinson suggests that the Government should initiate a comprehensive anti-poverty programme in at least one inner city area. If such a commitment were forthcoming from the Government, Peter Brinson suggests that the Foundations should back the Government's programme by one of their own. In his essay (see page 130) he sketches in the sort of programmes of action to which the Foundations could lend their support, and in doing so he sounds a rallying call for a renaissance of cultural, social and political activity in the inner city.

What part can schools play in this process of inner city renewal? In the first place the conferences were concerned to improve the education received by school children. The final chapter in this book introduces the reader to the range of experiments which the Gulbenkian Foundation has itself fostered in order to achieve the Greek goal of educating the whole man. The conferences were in little doubt as to how to achieve this on a much wider scale; schools would have to be much more outward-looking and community-based than many of them now are. Moreover, at present when the staff and pupils in secondary schools are at what can only be described as a 'low ebb', it is vital that successes in education should be publicised as quickly and widely as possible. Emphasis was therefore placed during part of the conference discussions on determining the best means of spreading news about success.

It is on this front that the Gulbenkian Foundation could make an important contribution. Eric Midwinter (see page 126) talked of establishing a centre to which teachers could come and participate in some of the new successes in secondary education before returning to their own schools. There would also be a need for such a centre to spread information both on television and by the printed word. In his paper, Peter Brinson recalls that some delegates drew attention to the need for a watchdog body on urban education. Such an organisation could encompass the role envisaged by Eric Midwinter as well as acting as spokesman with parents, teachers, pupils and other educational interests in the inner city. With cuts in public expenditure being made into the foreseeable future, and with the need to debate the distribution of resources between the inner city and the expanding new towns, what is to happen to the schooling and life changes of inner city children will have to be discussed within the context of this broader debate.

It might also be possible for such an urban education unit to take on two other activities. One very strong theme in many of the discussions at the two conferences was the need to equip today's pupils with skills which will allow them to choose some of the better paid jobs which sometimes go unfilled at present. There is a need for those responsible for the curriculum within schools to take account of the changing demands of the urban labour market. Many of the teachers at the conferences were only too well aware of this need, but asked where they could gain the necessary information. One additional function of the urban education unit might be to initiate the dialogue on how to relate school and work more effectively.

If the unit were generously funded it should undertake experiments of its own which, if successful, could then be taken up by Government. One very real problem in many inner city schools is what can usefully be done with some pupils after they have reached the age of 14. The urban education unit might consider financing an experiment which would allow pupils in one school to opt for part-time tutoring at the age of 14. Under present Education Acts pupils have to receive a minimum of four hours' education a day. This could easily be covered by part-time education. Those children who opt for part-time education and part-time work experience should be allowed to. At the age of 16 generous allowances on top of any educational maintenance allowances could be paid to those who continue in part-time education up to the age of 18. The unit would carefully monitor the effect of such a scheme both in the acquisition of educational skills, the general atmosphere of the school before and during the experiment, as well as the reactions of pupils, parents, teachers and employers. The full arguments in support of this and similar initiatives are set out in the following pages.

1
The Emerging Urban Crisis

The Calouste Gulbenkian Foundation called two conferences around the theme 'Education and the Urban Crisis' because it believed that the problems faced by cities were becoming more acute and that in an important respect the education system was not only failing to respond to these problems but adding to them. In this first chapter we attempt to answer the question: what fundamental changes are occurring in our inner cities? Alan Little begins our discussion by commenting that when most people in this country talk of an urban crisis, the picture they have in their minds is the newsreel shots of the violence and dislocation shown in American cities. He goes on to ask whether British cities will go the way of their American counterparts. He shows that in a number of important respects there are substantial racial differences between the two countries. However, minority groups in this country are drawing from American experience and in this way the course of events in American cities may become increasingly relevant to our own society.

1 American cities: a prototype for Britain? *Alan N. Little*

How far does the current American urban racial situation provide a portent for the United Kingdom? Initially it is important to point out the differences between the two situations. First, there is the question of size. Clearly there is no comparison of the relative size and concentrations of racial minority populations between the United Kingdom and USA. Well over 20 million Americans are black and this is more than one American in eight or nine, compared with an estimated $1\frac{1}{2}$ million 'coloured' in the United Kingdom, or less than 3 per cent of the population. Many American cities are

13

expecting that well over half their population will be black by the mid 1980s (and the list includes areas like metropolitan New York, Chicago, Philadelphia, St Louis, Detroit, Cleveland, Baltimore, Oakland and New Orleans), and already Washington DC, Newark and Gary have metropolitan populations of over 50 per cent black. Public school populations of most of these cities are already half black, and in Washington DC less than one pupil in 20 in the public schools is white. (Public schools in the States are equivalent to our maintained schools.) This contrasts with the United Kingdom: it was impossible a decade ago to find even census enumeration districts that were exclusively black, and currently only two of our local education authorities have more than one-quarter of their pupils defined as 'immigrant', and a further four between one-fifth and one-quarter classified in the same way. Although two out of three West Indian children are in schools in the Greater London area and half in the inner city area (ILEA) few schools have concentrations of the minority groups implied in the US figure. In the ILEA area 60 per cent of the so-called immigrant pupils are in schools with less than 20 per cent immigrants and only one immigrant pupil in six is in a school with over 50 per cent immigrants. In the whole country less than 150 schools had more than 50 per cent of their pupils defined as immigrant in 1971.

The second difference is the homogeneity of the American black population. Although the US minority population is not exclusively Negro, during recent discussions about both race and urban problems the difficulties of Puerto Rican and Asian as well as European immigrants have been given little emphasis. By contrast the United Kingdom settler population is highly differentiated. Using education figures of 270,450 pupils defined as 'immigrant' in 1971, 40 per cent were of West Indian origin, 20 per cent Indian, 10 per cent Pakistani and a further 10 per cent from Africa; all of these groups would be defined currently as black. The importance of this point is that the reasons the parents of these children had for coming to this country, the experiences they brought with them and their adjustment or maladjustment to the host environment are different. Of particular significance is the extent to which they bring with them a transferable and viable culture of their own, different to and independent of the dominant white culture. Certainly the African and Asian populations have their own cultural identity even in the United Kingdom, which contrasts markedly with the disorganised situations of many American blacks, whose culture is largely that of the dominant and rejecting white majority. How far the settlers from the Caribbean have an autonomous cultural identity and how far they are in a similar position to the American Negro is debatable. But even in the USA it is misleading to treat the black community as a one-dimensional group of people. To quote Downs:

> In reality, each racial ghetto contains a tremendous variety of persons who exhibit widely differing attitudes toward almost every question. Many are very poor, but just as many are not. Many have radical views – especially young people; many others are quite conservative – especially the older people. Many are 'on welfare' but many more are steadily employed. This diversity means that public policy concerning any given ghetto problem cannot be successful if it is aimed or based upon the attitudes and desires of only one group of persons affected by that problem, and a second widely prevalent oversimplification of ghetto problems is concentration of remedial action upon a single substandard condition. For instance, improving the deplorable housing conditions in many slums would not in itself eliminate most of the de-humanizing forces which operate there. In fact, no single category of programs can possibly be adequate to cope with the tangled problems that exist in ghettos. Any effective ghetto-improvement strategy must concern itself with at least jobs and employment, education, housing, health, personal safety, crime prevention, and income maintenance for dependent persons.

This quotation indicates the extent to which the American black population is differentiated both by its resources and by its problems and inevitably requires a variety of types of social action. Similarly recent settlers to the United Kingdom must be internally differentiated. Initially (and sensibly) it is possible to distinguish them by country of origin, but even these national origins are cut across by rural and urban differences, class and colour distinctions even in their country of origin. The Asian population provides an example of this diversity, but no less important are the differences between settlers from the West Indian islands, and even within islands immigrants from rural and urban areas and with different shades of blackness have different attitudes towards their own and other people's skin colour.

The history of immigrant groups in both American and British cities provides the third major difference between the two countries. The American black is an internal migrant, until a generation or two ago the inferior member of the southern plantation society. Migration to the cities was always a way out of a social system that in many respects paralleled caste society with the blacks being universally considered second-class citizens. Industrialisation in the northern cities and the war economy enormously widened the opportunities for the black population and chances for migrating north. But in essence many of the urban blacks are still living in the shadow of the slave plantations, in a way that settlers in the United Kingdom have never been dominated by the cultural and economic standards of the whites. Even in the West Indies domination of blacks by whites was never as severe as that in the USA (one illustration of this is that some of the leaders of recent black militantism in the USA had their origins not in the ghettos of the American cities nor in the American south but in the West Indies) and a major reason for this was that the whites both in the West Indies and in Asia were always outnumbered by the blacks. As a result a black bourgeoisie was always in evidence. Further, a peculiar mixture of missionary zeal and transient colonial exploitation gave the relationship between whites and blacks in the West Indies a different flavour from its counterpart in the USA. The capacity of the Asian cultures to withstand the pressures of commercial, political and religious colonisation is legendary; resilience is a word that has frequently been used to describe the capacity of Asians to preserve a cultural integrity and identity against colonisation. As a result the settlers in the United Kingdom do not present the same kind or degree of cultural disorganisation or perhaps the same need to see themselves through white eyes and standards as do American blacks. The term American blacks was an apt description of the situation of the Negro in the USA, in a way that black or brown British is not accurate for the first generation of settlers in the United Kingdom.

A further difference between the countries is the institutional framework within which race relations take place and which structures the economy and social opportunities and life styles of minority populations. The different relationship between central, regional and local authorities in the USA and the United Kingdom inevitably means that problems and opportunities differ. The fact that nearly one-third of housing in the United Kingdom is controlled by public bodies and is therefore within the public domain means that the public policy (in this case local authority policy) could (if we wanted it to) have a profound effect on the housing opportunities of smaller and minority groups. The fact that the state is a major employer not only in the bureaucratic sense of the civil service but directly in industrial sectors like mines, public utilities and steel, and in services like transport, posts and telecommunications, means that public recruitment, training and promotion policies could directly change the employment situation of minorities and serve as an example to private employers. Finally, parallel with the migration control of the 1960s came a legal framework for race relations. This included legislation against incitement to race hatred and discrimination in employment, housing and recreational facilities; and the creation of a framework for the encouragement of harmonious community relations. The positive effort to discourage discrimination was established within a decade of the arrival of sizeable numbers of black settlers in this country. This contrasts with the USA, where legislation and action against discrimination and inequality were imposed upon set conventions and behaviour that had been established generations previously. One further point should be made: one element in any judgment of both the urban and the racial situation is the way people define their situation. It is possible to argue that because of differences in scale, history, homogeneity and institutional framework, comparisons of the racial situations in the United Kingdom and the USA are unlikely to be helpful. Nevertheless, if people, especially activists in this situation, believe lessons can be drawn in the light of these comparisons, then a different situation is being created. Here an obvious example is the way in which many members of minority communities see parallels of their situation with that of the USA and accept either the rhetoric or the tactics of American blacks for the UK situation. Academic analysis suggesting the inappropriateness of such identifications will not stop them being made or their influence on actual behaviour. It seems to me that perhaps the most potent way in which the American racial situation may influence that of the UK is in the lessons minority group members are drawing from American experience. Perhaps the slogan of students during the 1960s, 'Berkeley yesterday, LSE today, where tomorrow?' is an illustration of this point: suggestions of ways in which American universities differed from British did not stop students in the latter emulating the former.

2 What's happening in the inner city?

Discussion now turns to what is happening in our inner cities. David Eversley highlights three trends which are making for an increasing segregation of the poor. The first has been the migration from the inner city of more able working-class families. This has resulted in a rise in the proportion of poor and handicapped people remaining in the inner city. Dr Eversley estimates that something like 30 per cent of the people living in inner London are dependent on means-tested benefits and that this proportion is growing. Second, not only have planning policies creamed off many of the more able inner city inhabitants, but regional development policy has meant that fewer capital resources have been available for inner city areas. The third trend discussed in the following section is the way our education policy is adding to the problems of the inner city. Dr Eversley notes that one of the principal disadvantages of inner city education stems from its weak links with the urban labour market. The education system appears intent on endowing school leavers with skills which are of little or no use in today's labour market, let alone the labour market twenty years hence when today's school leaver will be in mid-career. This theme is developed further in Chapter 4.

(a) Segregating the poor *David Eversley*

We have heard much about the urban crisis, of which the crisis in education is supposed to be an integral part. It is thought that the failure of the educational system is in itself one of the main causes of the perpetuation of the cycle of poverty and deprivation. Moreover the victims of the typical environment of the inner city present almost insurmountable problems to the educationalist. Yet I doubt if there is such a thing as an 'urban crisis'. It is a journalistic catch-phrase used to draw attention to conditions which have always existed and which, if anything, are now less acute than they once were, but which have come into prominence again because of the slowing down, or even reversal, of that long process of economic growth to which we all once looked to dispose of the remnants of squalor and suffering. The 'crisis' is nothing but a point in time when familiar conditions suddenly present themselves as being beyond the capacity of our present system to remedy, or at least to ameliorate. If we do not adopt new policies then some very unpleasant consequences might follow, but then again this is not a state of affairs confined to a 'crisis'. To pursue a medical analogy: the patient is not only acutely ill so that immediate intervention is required; but he is also chronically sick, which requires a course of prolonged treatment to get at the fundamental causes of his condition. It may be critical whether we decide to do one thing or another, but the wrong choice does not necessarily produce catastrophe; it may only prolong unacceptable conditions.

We must certainly accept that the changes in income levels and income distributions are crucial, because personal disposable incomes are in the long run the only source of acceptable determinants of living standards, as opposed to emergency allocations of housing or a school bussing scheme. This, again, is not new: it has been at the core of all discussions about social policy ever since the first taxes were levied for social purposes, as opposed to the 'hand-outs of conventional charity'. It is fashionable today to say that the income or wealth distribution is unchanged since 1860, 1900, 1950 and even 1960. It is always possible to juggle the statistics one way or another. But there are some very basic measures that one must look at. With some exceptions they show changes for the better, even between 1960 and 1970. One of these measures is the inter-quartile range in our tables of income distribution. This shows that the size of the gap between the upper quartile (the top 25 per cent of all income earners) and the lower quartile (the bottom 25 per cent) has narrowed quite appreciably, with the interesting exception of London in the last few years. Here this gap appears to have widened. However, it would be wrong to talk in terms of rich and poor. The upper 25 per cent consist of households whose income is now more than about £60 per week, and most of them cannot be called rich by any stretch of the imagination.

Thus, overall, the distribution of money incomes is more equal than it was. This is due to a variety of factors, of which the taking of money from the better-off in taxes and redistributing it to the worst-off in the form of allowances, pensions and grants is only a part. The increasing proportion of the population who are salaried work-ers, who neither receive wages nor are self-employed, nor live off unearned incomes, has helped to bring about a more progressive equalisation of real incomes. However, the concentration of people in a spatial sense sometimes serves to show inequalities more clearly than the national statistics, especially the contrast between the low real incomes of large groups in the inner city, as opposed to the high and rising incomes of people in outer suburbia and the various regional growth zones. A great deal of our misunderstandings have arisen because we have discussed the matter as if narrowing the after-tax income between the best-off and the worst-off is in itself a cure of evils: it is no more than a step in the right direction, and it is perfectly compatible with a number of other phenomena which we perceive as aggravations; for example the spatial concentration of certain types of poverty and deprivation, and an increase in social and community tensions.

In Britain London, Glasgow, Birmingham and Liverpool are the most important examples of cities where lower incomes are in-creasingly evident amongst a shrinking inner metropolitan popula-tion. It should be noted that these are quite different cities. But to distinguish between these cities is merely to say that poverty and deprivation are easier (or more difficult) to bear when they occur in an environment of general deprivation (or prosperity). The factors leading to the out-migration of the more skilled, socially more mobile, salaried and professional workers with their progressive incomes, are well known. The accelerating and rather unbalanced outflow of population, against which we argued at the Greater London Development Plan Inquiry, is critical in that it leads to relatively larger concentrations of relatively more disadvantaged people in the inner city. They may not be worse off now than they would have been if the others had remained in the city, but they are certainly no better off. Unfortunately the Layfield Panel, and many planners, still believe that to empty the city of a quarter or half its population will make those who stay behind better off. Of course this is not so. Some of the people we have been talking about at this conference live in conditions of considerable distress at very high densities. Although the out-movement of population was supposed to give more room to everybody, we have in fact built dwellings of ever-increasing height. This is not the place to expound the reasons why this has occurred but we must not assume that we shall all get more space and other resources to the poorest by removing the better-off from their midst. The demand for community schools may in part stem from the fact that as more and more people have left the city, so the education authorities find it uneconomical to keep open all the secondary schools in rapidly depopulating areas. They concentrate children into the larger, once-fashionable comprehensive schools where all needs can perhaps be met more easily, but at the cost of making children go further to school than was formerly the custom in the inner areas, and by progressively breaking the link between home and school (although it is open to speculation how strong this link was). So we see that a shrinking city brings a whole host of new problems, as well as making old ones stand out more sharply. If, at the end of another ten years of present trends, London has fewer than 5 million people, of whom a high proportion are poor, old, black, handicapped or have prison records, then there will be many voices heard claiming that deprivation has become worse. It is possible that what is in fact a residue, left over after the rise in affluence has brought its benefits to the great majority, will form an unbroken mass of poverty in certain areas – unbroken even by the process of 'gentrification' which affects only relatively small parts of the inner city. In other words, we are not dealing here with national aggregates. Even if it can be shown that, in a situation of slow overall economic growth but accelerating inflation, there are quite large sections of the community whose bargaining power has enabled them to maintain or even improve their incomes, the fact will still remain that such improvements may have been bought at the expense of more concentrated impoverishment for substantial sections of the population elsewhere.

This process of relative concentration of the deprived in the inner city is aggravated by national government policies which put more resources into growth areas. Growth pays, and is paid for. We are led to believe that because cities are losing population, they no longer merit massive investment in the infrastructure. Great efforts have been made in development areas with the very pleasing result that by 1970 median incomes in Monmouthshire and West Lothian were the same, in money terms, as in London. In real terms this means higher income than London. This is a great success, but it also illustrates the plight of London. The tragedy is that it is not only public but private investment which follows success and growth.

So when we consider developments in the inner city we need to consider not only the question of education and job opportunities, but also of improvements to the environment, to amenities, to the social and economic infrastructure. All these things are improving for large groups of the population; but they are standing still or getting worse for smaller groups. Deprivation seems to mean not being on the receiving end of the rising 'flood' of private and public largesse. Naturally, if for economic reasons this 'flood' is no longer rising in real terms, the situation deteriorates. When the general situation becomes worse, increases for the people at the margin of existence mean that they have the right to apply for more means-tested benefits. But if the benefit scales are themselves inadequate, or fail to catch up with rising prices, or if they are so structured as to reduce the chances of 'take-up', then even this right is illusory and does not result in an improved standard of living. Alternatively it may simply be that a group which has until recently on the whole maintained its living standards, is put at a disadvantage by some new development. The decline in manufacturing industry has been affecting London for a long time and until recently this trend had few adverse results, for labour was rapidly absorbed elsewhere into fairly well-paid jobs. This may now have ceased.

Some analysts of the present position have in fact made the more general observation that many of Britain's balance of payments and regional policies have tended to confer more benefit on foreign capital and foreign labour, especially by way of creation of better-paid technical and managerial jobs in the new sectors, than on the indigenous population. This is normally attributed to the evil machinations of the multi-national or monopolistic firms concerned. But it is equally plausible to say that any economic revival in Britain, were it to create a mass of new good job opportunities, would lead to an increased influx of people from other countries who have the skill, the capacity for sustained hard work, and the willingness to go where the work is located. If that were so, it would indeed be a striking condemnation both of our educational and our housing policies. The excuse that our best hands and brains emigrate will not do. If the products of our vocational, technical and general education system were suited to fill the vacancies created by growth (where this does occur), they would not emigrate, nor would their potential employers go to the trouble of importing personnel from abroad.

One should not blame this kind of social problem of the inner city on the inadequacies of any one service, whether education, housing or employment promotion. Much of it is due to the excessive success, if we can call it that, of successive governments' inter-regional and intra-regional policies. These policies have increased economic prospects in some of the poorer regions, and have created tidy and prosperous growth areas in the south-east region, but are making life increasingly difficult now for the old large cities. I say this with hindsight, because I spent many years of my life promoting what we used to call 'overspill', and the founding of new towns. But we did not then see what would happen to the populations that were left behind in the cities; the people who could not, or would not, move. It is amongst them that our worst problems are to be found. This has already become a self-reinforcing cycle of deprivation of which education is just one aspect. People who are dependent for their rent on the DHSS are not usually viewed as good tenants by housing managers, whether in new towns or anywhere else. And it is amongst the unskilled that we find those who are least able to pay their rents. The *General Household Survey* has demonstrated again the strong association between low occupational status and long absences from work through sickness – another two-way link in the chain in which poor educational attainment, inadequate housing and poverty all figure. All these people are concentrated in the inner city, not in rural areas or suburbia. In the aftermath of several years of strong pressure on new towns to accept at least a proportion of people who do not quite conform to their original image of model citizens, a few families have been granted tenancies on other than employment grounds. But it amounts to a negligible contribution.

It has been suggested that one of the remedies against this sort of concentration of casualties and potential casualties in certain parts of the inner city is to encourage the better-off to return to areas where they once lived, and perhaps even to settle in traditional old working-class districts. This has already been happening, though on a much smaller scale than is often assumed. It leads to cries of 'gentrification' and allegations that planners are deliberately robbing the poor of their habitations to make way for the rich. However far-fetched the suggestion may have sounded at the time, the 1969 Housing Act was used deliberately to reduce the stock of housing available to poorer tenants, and there can be no doubt that landlords attempted to obtain vacant possession by one means or another, though not, by the early 1970s, through Rachmanite tactics. Most improvement grants went to owner-occupiers, or local authorities, and many of those that were awarded to private owners resulted in genuine additions to the housing stock. Moreover in many, if not most cases (at least in the more conscientious London boroughs), tenants were properly rehoused. And in the long run we do not even know whether the return of some better-off groups to these neglected areas may not in the end make a contribution to the rehabilitation of the inner city.

Let me summarise the points I have made in this section. All the evidence we have on incomes and employment, on housing and education, on migration and social structure, points to the fact that, as the result of certain universally agreed planning policies, the inner city has been put at a tremendous disadvantage. Moreover the future looks gloomy. Entry into the EEC can only accelerate the decline of manufacturing industry and, coupled with our continuing regional policy, this will hit hardest the manual worker in the Midlands and the south-east. The nil growth in real incomes will aggravate this position. If growth does cease, the main burden of stagnation will be borne by those who are already poor, and the young unskilled. They will be deprived of what prospects they have come to expect within the traditional structure. In the past all amelioration has depended on redistribution. Without growth there has rarely been redistribution, except under the exigencies of wartime. One can only redistribute the surplus growth. This seems to be a fact of life under our type of government. No administration will ever have the courage to take away from what Ray Pahl calls the 'middle mass' that which they already have, as opposed to a proportion of that which is added to their living standards each year. When I made these remarks at the conference they were treated with amused incredulity. Since then the decline in real income has begun, and we may confidently predict that in another year or two the opponents of growth will also realise that the poorest have been the first to suffer.

In this second section I intend to look at some of the trends already discernible within London. This accords closely with what planners are beginning to see: that the problem of scale is very relevant and that problems are simply not the same in smaller population concentrations as in large ones. In a way that was recognised the moment people began to agree with Ebenezer Howard, who believed that a garden city of 30,000 people must be a better place to live in than a megalopolis. But that is not the whole story. It is not simply a question of having the same problems in large cities as in small ones so that, multiplied together, they appear more formidable. It is rather that the large cities are the ones that are shrinking, while the proportion of people with problems is rising. At the same time the costs of maintaining the fabric of a large old city are rising. A very large increase in the *per capita* burdens is being borne by the remaining population. If London has only 5 million inhabitants by 1991, and that is most likely at the rate we are going, the proportion of multiply deprived households in that smaller total must rise quite drastically. At present perhaps not more than 10 per cent of all London households are multiply deprived. This percentage accounts for 260,000 families, enough to keep social workers very busy. But given a continuation of migration trends, continued failure to apply public services in the right place and at the right time, this 10 per cent could quite easily become 20 per cent. And this 20 per cent might be only part of a much larger army of Londoners who only manage to maintain the minimum decencies of life because they claim their means-tested benefits. In other words we shall have more people who will never rise above some arbitrarily laid down minimum standard. This proportion of Londoners may now be as high as 30 per cent, and it could rise to 50 per cent.

Not since the Diggers and Levellers has anybody really believed in absolute equality in this country. What we share is a tradition of a move *towards* equality. That is what Tawney taught the generation which followed him. And the speed of that movement is dictated by the sacrifice of their own advantage which the 'haves' can be persuaded to make in favour of the 'have-nots'. So long as that sacrifice is limited to a share of the extra standard of living which would have accrued to the better-off during a period of growth, it becomes a question of judging the 'nicely more or less' of the level of taxation. But if there is a real fall in the standard of living even of the better-off, as in the depression of the 1930s, the axe will fall on the dole. We now know that this is economically counterproductive. What we do not know is whether this would be politically feasible today.

In our state of ignorance about the extent of our own potential nobility I would be very chary of saying that the notion of equality is very deep-rooted, or that the present levels of public expenditure for social purposes are as yet sacrosanct. Equally we are ignorant about the social values we want our education system to instil. In this situation, it would seem best to continue to try to achieve further steps forward towards equality of income and opportunity, and especially esteem, and the elimination of those forms of discrimination against minorities which stand in the way of progress towards equality. We are, I think, committed to this path, even though we do not know whether in a period of economic stagnation we can persuade the electorate that the process must go on. And we must learn to accept that with this process must go ever-increasing free choice. This must apply to the recipients of the bonanza of social and health services and education, as for the man who has earned all his income. People should be able to do what they like with what they receive; rent 23 inch colour television sets, smoke themselves into lung cancer, or read pornography. Since Richard Hoggart we have learned to live with our fate in this respect.

I am guilty of the same failure as everyone else in this discussion in talking about deprivation. I have not defined what the word means, nor whether the expression is absolute or relative. I want to avoid the idea of relative deprivation. I therefore accept that there are people, especially children, who are deprived in an absolute sense, not just, for instance, children who perform less than optimally in schools (see page 4). Deprived children most frequently come from deprived families. They lack in their environment, their food, their clothing, their recreational opportunities, and perhaps their family life, goods, services, feelings and sensations which we regard as crucial to the full development of a future healthy adult in our society.

Who are these families who produce these deprived children? They are not of course a static element. If in ten years there are still a quarter of a million multiply deprived families in London, they will not be all the same as the present ones, or their children. A large city attracts, holds or expels a large shifting population of people who must either move or see in a move a marginal chance of bettering themselves. Better-off people are not usually forced to move, and only do so if they see a great advantage in income, status or environment. In the excessive mobility of the very poor (leading to frequent changes in schooling) lies a root cause of deprivation itself. Instability is an inbuilt feature. There is a cycle of deprivation which is not necessarily an inherited trait passed from mother to daughter, but obviously a child brought up in a succession of poor environments will find it difficult to break out of them. It is a self-reinforcing process. But the cycle is also spatial: deprivation is attached to a type of dwelling which by definition attracts only the deprived, and so probably disadvantages them further. The components of the deprived groups are not exactly known. They include those with small incomes, and the old, but not all the old have small incomes, and not all people with small incomes are necessarily deprived. There are more large households which are deprived than small ones, but there is no absolute rule. On the whole larger households have larger incomes, mostly because they contain more earners, and because of social benefits. But the additional earners may be wives who ought to look after their children, or children who ought still to be at school.

There are other groups, more easily recognisable: the one-parent families, the disabled, the chronically sick, the households where there is a father in theory, but he is away, or in prison, or unemployed, or just a bad provider (who exercises his choice not to give his wife enough housekeeping). Then there are those who are discriminated against, mainly the immigrants, but also the ex-prisoners, and women with illegitimate children, and perhaps even ex-dockers who, it is said, are now finding it difficult to get jobs because of their reputation for militancy.

How does this multiple deprivation manifest itself? We have no agreed set of criteria or social indicators. Everybody manufactures his own arbitrary and subjective definition. The most common feature is probably bad environment, and especially poor access to services, amenities and facilities which most of us take for granted. Hence it seems to follow that the larger the area in which deprivation is already rife, the more difficult access becomes. If an area is poorly served, whether by schools or doctors or libraries or shops, people who are mobile and wish to make choices move out. Newcomers then move in, and the faster this process goes on, the less likely it is that better facilities will be created, either in the private or the public sector. It is the basic notion underlying attempts at 'social mix' that if more of the newcomers are better-off and already better educated they will exert greater effective demand for improved public and private facilities for the area.

It seems as if we are perpetuating in London a wide area of deprivation running roughly north-east from Hammersmith to South Camden and Islington and then east and south through

Hackney, as far out as Newham. And there is the counterpart of this tract in the south, running from Wandsworth to Greenwich. (Young and Willmott have portrayed these zones of deprivation not in the form of two arcs, but in the form of a 'cross' of poverty running north and south and east and west through the low-lying parts of London, intersecting somewhere east of Charing Cross.) Of course there are signs that the arc is being broken by odd pockets of colonisation by very well-off people. This does not amount to much, and will probably not continue, because the market for this sort of development is limited. It may change the character of very small areas, but not of this large tract. The most characteristic thing about such areas is not so much absolute squalor, but their monotony – the absence of green as well as buildings with much individuality. The trained sociologist can, of course, perceive differentiated patterns and local nuances. The presence of immigrants also helps to break the feeling of drab sameness. But there is less choice in the shops, on library shelves, or on the menus of cafés. Take the library. The exceptional boy (or girl) at the local school (if not already 'creamed off' by the meritocratic process) cannot get the special book recommended to him, or cultivate his taste by browsing in the local library. The nearest bookshop with anything other than pulp fiction is a 15p bus ride away. The private sector provides nothing but what local incomes will steadily demand – the bare essentials, plus the traditional extravagances of the poor (in middle-class value systems): beer, tobacco, betting. There may be old public baths, and a small old-fashioned park, and certainly fish and chip shops. But the leisure and recreation potential of that area is still geared to the past, and to poverty.

Large numbers of families in these areas are trapped into poverty. However hard these people work, increases in earnings are matched by a reduction of means-tested benefits. In other words the net income of the household does not rise. The poverty trap occurs at a level of income between £30 and £50, depending on rents, the journey to work, the number of children, or the presence of invalids.

The exceptionally gifted child will probably break out of this environment. We have heard a lot about D. H. Lawrence. This is the fiction of Richard Llewellyn and Dennis Potter and all the other authors who have made good, and those who haven't written books but have made the grade from squalor to great affluence. But the ability to persist in one's schooling and self-improvement to the point where one can break out under one's own steam is a relatively infrequent phenomenon, and as the inner city becomes poorer, so at once the difficulties increase. Why is there such high unemployment amongst male school leavers of West Indian parentage? Why is there said to be a high degree of delinquency amongst them? Is it inherent genetically, is it prejudice, is it their environment, is it the whole atmosphere of discouragement and past defeat which has set up this cycle? What is astonishing is not that some take the 'easy' way out and resort to petty theft and fraud, but that such behaviour is not more widespread. When we were the 'other ranks' in the army we made quite sure we also shared privileges given to some of the officers. We were not at all scrupulous about the way we obtained extra leave, better food, and more home comforts in our billets. In wartime this was accepted practice. In London, in 1975, it is anti-social behaviour to take what most people seem to have got, and what is denied to you because of the colour of your skin, or your school record, or the street in which you live. The underpaid postman who does a second, moonlighting job and does not pay tax on it, is working hard to get himself out of the primary poverty to which his public employment condemns him. But what he does, out of necessity, neither promotes family life nor inculcates respect for our tax laws. And the same goes for the youngsters who do part-time jobs. Where is the boundary between the admirable thrift of the underpaid newspaper boy and the punishable activities of whatever the modern equivalent of the bookie's runner may be? The professional middle classes can supplement their income in the same way, and with impunity. Of course tax evasion is much more widespread in the upper income ranges. Unless the right policies are adopted (and some have been touched upon in this paper) the inner city will increasingly become the domain of the poor. It is here that we see the seeds of an urban crisis, if there is one at all.

Last, I should now like to examine the pressures these developments in the inner city will place upon the education system. Underlying our discussions has been the assumption that children in certain areas are deprived because they do not attain some particular standard at school-leaving age and this is due to their environment, or the inadequacy of the education process itself. One of their principal disadvantages stems from the fact that the education system is so poorly linked to the urban economy, and more particularly to the labour market. Children from some schools never stay beyond the MSLA. They do not have any meaningful further education because there are simply no jobs for the less gifted children that offer career prospects. Let me give just one example. London is losing its manufacturing industries and so one traditional avenue to at least a moderately decent standard of living is increasingly closed to school leavers. As Peter Hall and John Vaizey note on page 32 and page 34 growth is specially evident in two fields: offices (administration and commercial), and service industries linked to tourism and allied activities. Yet it seems as if the unskilled school child is condemned to work in the transport industries, in the most junior clerical occupations, and in semi-skilled jobs in distribution, which offer neither currently high incomes nor future promotion prospects. On the other hand, the hotel and catering trade, for instance, has to recruit its highly paid chefs and pastry cooks from other countries. Offices find it impossible to recruit bilingual shorthand typists. Firms either are driven from London or recruit staff from abroad. Why should the London school system not turn out girls who can read and write their own language, and then learn a second language well enough to write it in both shorthand and on a machine? This is not beyond the capacity of an 11-year education process, with modern teaching aids, a surplus of language teachers, and the possibility of a little expenditure on sending students abroad to finish their schooling. And there is no need for technical colleges to turn out only canteen managers and school meals cooks. If local authorities were willing to arrange it, even boys who are not much good at spelling could learn to be good cooks.

These are just two rather obvious examples. But the main fact is that the London labour market is crying out for people with particular skills. And this demand has been foreseen for a long time in many cases. Yet the education system is slow to adapt itself. The decline of London as the primary international financial and commercial centre of Western Europe could be halted if, amongst other things, there were an adequate supply of suitable office labour.

We have here a typical dilemma of our times. Offices are 'bad' in the primitive language of self-styled radicals. London is losing manufacturing industry. Service jobs are badly paid, and the future of tourism is, to say the least, uncertain. What has emerged however is that despite inflation, unemployment, chronic balance of payments crises, etc., London is still highly regarded as the centre of the world's trade in 'invisibles'. Yet there are many who would rather like to kill this one growth sector, and thus deprive the London school leaver of his last hope of local employment. Meanwhile, by restricting new office building in the way successive governments and County Hall administrations have done, they have not only reduced long-term prospects but actually increased monopoly profits and helped near-bankrupt developers out of their difficulties. After the office market reached the peak of its boom in 1972/3, and rents had soared to prohibitive levels, a reduction of activity set in, more firms took their offices out of London, and soon a surplus of space was created. This led, in due course, to a great mass of unfinished or unoccupied buildings, as well as millions of square feet of unused planning permissions. So of course rents began to fall towards levels where, in due course, we might have seen a revival of London's activity and therefore better employment chances for school leavers. But at this precise moment authority (one must assume owing to pressure exercised equally by the property lobby and the radical left, acting in unison) announced that it would again stop all building, until rents would start to rise again because of the shortage of space (which is synonymous with loss of job prospects). One cites this example in order to counter those who always find single and simple solutions for our complex social problems.

Of course it is not true that if we ensure that 75 per cent of all school leavers in every part of the country are trained for office jobs, they will automatically obtain good, progressive jobs when they are ready for the labour market. But I do say that given the very well-established long-term fall in jobs in manufacturing industry, and especially those of an unskilled or semi-skilled kind, and the rise in the number of jobs in offices, laboratories, educational, administrative and professional services, it is odd that our education system should still be geared to the output of skills which are not even current in today's labour demand, never mind the sort of situation we are going to have by the time today's school leavers are in mid-career. The question of educational deprivation which we have been discussing obscures this other subject. We assume that the poverty cycle can be blamed simply on poor environment and bad schools in the early years. At least as great a part of the total trouble might well be the failure of the education system to be thoroughly integrated with our planning of production of goods and services: volume, skills and location.

John Vaizey centres our discussion on the employment prospects in the inner city if the British economy continues to grow at its historic growth rate for the remainder of this century. Compared with other countries our economy's rate of growth is very slow; but even so, by the year 2000 we shall almost see the disappearance of workers involved in what are called the extractive industries and a considerable fall in the numbers employed in the manufacturing industry, and a large rise in service employment. Vaizey notes that these changes will make it even more difficult for students of inner city schools to gain and keep employment. Moreover, this continual decline of the inner city will give rise to a growing proportion of children coming from home circumstances that are usually identified as a major cause of educational difficulties.

(b) The urban economy *John Vaizey*

In a quarter of a century great changes occur. It is just over thirty years since the 1944 Education Act was passed. Since then over 7 million houses and flats have been built; over three-quarters of the children are in new or remodelled schools; most students in higher education are in post-war buildings. Over the next quarter-century, even at the present inadequate rate of house building, 10 million houses and flats will be built, and all the schools now existing would be replaced if school building kept up.

The first thing that Colin Leicester's study on projected growth rates of the economy shows is that at any rate of growth between $2\frac{1}{2}$ and 3 per cent (which is the historic rate of British growth), the year 2001 will be by present standards a year of great prosperity. Of course disaster (like a war) might strike. Nor is the balance of payments likely to be a major constraint on growth at that rate. 'Prosperity' could mean many things. It could mean more and more cars and more and more traffic jams. Or it could mean more and more parks, swimming pools, golf courses and theatres. But what it certainly does mean is that poverty will only exist because the will and the machinery to end it are not there; the measures to end it already exist.

Let us take Leicester's 'middle' forecast (he made high, medium and low forecasts) which is that consumption will grow by 2·9 per cent a year between 1969 and 2001. (It has already grown faster than that.) In 1958 £p, this means housing expenditure will triple, durable goods will nearly triple, as will recreational goods; motoring will go up by five times; entertainment will more than double. But government expenditure is likely to rise by 3·2 per cent a year, which implies a fivefold increase in education outlays and a tripling of expenditure in the National Health Service.

These are not firm predictions. They merely point out what the law of compound interest does to the national income over thirty years or so.

But, and this is the second point, these massive changes mean not only prosperity, but major alterations in the pattern of jobs. We have to recall that all Britain's basic industries (coal, agriculture, steel, railways) have raised productivity and made hundreds of thousands of people redundant since 1945. This process will continue. In 1969 over 1·17 million people worked in 'extractive' industries; by the year 2001 this is likely to be 300,000. In 1969 9½ million people worked in manufacturing. By 2001 this will be under 6 million. On the other hand, employment in 'services' will rise from 11 million to nearly 17 million. It is this massive shift in the labour market that spells serious trouble for inner city areas, so dependent on unskilled and semi-skilled jobs for manual labour in manufacturing industries, and jobs like those in the docks, which are just disappearing. Unless a serious attempt is made to train people for the new types of employment, then unemployment will be endemic. The dole might be generous, but life on the dole is what America's urban crisis is largely about.

The consequences of this change of economic structure on the demand for unskilled manual labour are self-evident. It is highly probable that the products of inner city schools will find it hard to gain and keep employment. This is a matter of grave educational concern.

There is another matter which deserves attention, and indeed may be crucial, and that is the distribution of income. I have dealt with the problems of inequality at greater length elsewhere (see for example *Whatever Happened to Equality?* ed. John Vaizey, BBC Publications, 1975) but certain points in addition to those made by David Eversley (see page 19) need to be revived. While the general level of income per head has risen dramatically since 1900 – by any measure – the spread of incomes has only narrowed since 1950. There seems likely to be some social mechanism which constantly throws out at the bottom, as it were, a predetermined proportion of poorly paid people. The greater part of this poverty is relative rather than absolute (Virginia Woolf's country cottage would count as a slum today for instance); but absolute poverty continues, even in wealthy countries. It is also the case that the greater part of this poverty is associated with old age, chronic ill-health and children. But the link between these forms of poverty is low pay and intermittent employment. It is improbable that – in the absence of a substantial programme of successful social engineering – this condition will be reduced, and because this social group is excessively located (statistically speaking) in the inner city areas, and some of its families are larger than average, while others are one-parent families, and its background (socially and possibly genetically) is so deprived, it follows that a serious educational problem will continue to be associated with it.

Thus, casting a cold eye over the possible course of the economy over the next thirty years, two conclusions emerge. The first is that if economic change continues (and there is little reason to suppose that it will not despite our present difficulties), there will be a substantial growth in the kinds of economic structures that now dominate, let us say, the borough of Barnet, and the county of Westmorland, the one lived in by doctors and directors, and the other containing country cottages and retired parents, which will then lead to the sort of social and educational structures now existing in suburban New York, and the canton of Zurich. On the other hand, it is difficult not to see a further deterioration in inner city areas, following a further process of depopulation, a growing difficulty in finding employment, and a rise in the proportion of children coming from home circumstances that have been identified as the major causes of educational difficulty. Reforms which will help the education system meet this growing challenge are outlined in Chapter 4.

Peter Hall develops our analysis of the consequences of the rise in service employment. He shows that some service employment demands a highly skilled workforce and is consequently very well paid. But most jobs in the service industries will be for unskilled workers and will be relatively poorly paid. David Eversley and John Vaizey have already pointed out that many people remaining in the inner city will be seeking unskilled employment. Peter Hall suggests that our most urgent task is to balance the employment prospects which are developing throughout metropolitan regions with the supply of skilled and often unskilled labour which is heavily concentrated in the inner city. Failure to do so will mean either moving out each day the unskilled inner city dweller to work opportunities in the surrounding areas or a massive increase in long-term unemployment of residents in the inner city.

(c) Planning employment *Peter Hall*

I should like to develop the analysis John Vaizey presents on the future employment prospects in the inner city. One can usefully divide the population in any advanced industrial country into three broad groups, in terms of the labour force and their dependants, with perhaps a sub-division of one of these. The first broad group is the manufacturing group, which can be sub-divided very crudely into a skilled group and a semi-skilled/unskilled group. Here is a special problem, which has hit this country with particular force in the last twenty years: the decline of certain occupations which were hitherto regarded as skilled. Jobs like coalmining, for instance;

dockwork; engine-driving on the railways; all were regarded as skilled jobs, but I think it is true to say that they have declined in terms of the skill that society thinks they need. Some of them have been affected by technological change; a job which was regarded as skilled, such as packing holds in ships, has been abolished by containerisation, so that we are seeing the death throes of a vast dock industry. And as John Vaizey has already noted, there is going to be a declining semi-skilled and unskilled sector in industry; one can assume that the status of these people is not going to improve, because those who remain in manufacturing are going to be used for very unskilled types of work. It will be the type of work that can be taught to people in only a few hours by intensive job-training techniques.

I should like to concentrate, however, on future developments in the service sector. Broadly, and rather crudely, it's possible to divide this sector into two parts representing two very different types of industry. First there is the very highly skilled managerial and professional division; education, mass communications, white-collar employment in a great variety of public and private corporations. This is the fastest growing sector of industry at present. It requires considerable formal general education and also in many cases increasingly specialised education. But it is the other type of service industry which should specially concern us: the unskilled sector. This has always been with us; it was of exceptional importance for instance in the mid-Victorian economy, both in cities and in the countryside.

It is still a very important source of employment in the backward rural areas of Britain – in mid-Wales for instance, which is one of the poorest parts of Great Britain. Mid-Wales has about three-quarters of its employment in services, but nearly all of it is of this very low-paid unskilled type. The interesting question is: what is the future of this type of industry? I believe that it may have a very considerable future, which may paradoxically give rise to problems. As the modern economy develops, and as more and more people pass into the skilled highly paid decision-making part of the service sector, they in turn create very large demands for relatively unskilled service labour: people who come and fix things in and around the house, people who perform routine tasks in offices, people who serve beer in pubs or serve at tables in restaurants, people above all who serve the tourist trade. The rise of the tourist industry is one of the most important aspects of the present-day economy: it is a development which is much further advanced in North America than in Western Europe as one may see from the vast scale of the hotel–motel–eating-out industry in the USA as compared with Great Britain and Western Europe. It makes a vast and increasing demand for very repetitive, very unprestigious labour which many people are reluctant to do and which doesn't allow much job satisfaction. This will give considerable problems unless some way can be found of giving these people a feeling of doing a satisfactory and competent job of work.

A common middle-class gripe we always hear in Britain is about the declining quality of public services, and this I think is partly associated with the fact that the people who might once have performed these services rather efficiently and intelligently have long ago been sucked up into more highly skilled, highly paid jobs. Thus you get a decline in what can be called the Mr Kipps phenomenon, the efficient shopkeeper. One of the major jobs of educational policy may be to cope with the demands of the economy for this sort of labour, to find a way of making it meaningful and interesting for the people who are going to perform it, and to find a way above all of giving it a certain prestige.

I am a geographer and I tend therefore to think of such problems in spatial terms. These demands for unskilled or semi-skilled service jobs will come in two parts. Some of them will be widely distributed across our urban areas. They are lcoal service employment tied to the demands of people in local residential areas and therefore very highly dispersed, especially in the higher income areas. The other sector of demand is concentrated in the centre of very large cities. Here it depends either upon the existence of demand during the day from the highly paid decision-makers – and this occurs in relatively few cities, the Londons and the New Yorks of this world – or upon certain basic industries, such as tourism, which happen in part to be concentrated in the centres of these same cities. The US experience however shows that even in a city like New York, which has a very high and concentrated demand for unskilled service employment in the city centre, this is insufficient to deal with the large numbers of people offering their skills (or the lack of skills) for such jobs. Here is a problem which is of the demands for unskilled labour migrating to the suburb, while the supply of unskilled labour remains concentrated in the centres of the cities.

I believe that there is a much greater similarity between British and US cities in their spatial evolution than has hitherto been thought. This is concealed to some extent by physical appearances; British cities don't look very like US cities owing to the operation of different systems of land use controls, but functionally they are very similar. British cities are decentralising populations very rapidly to their suburbs. Big English cities have lost up to 20 per cent of their population in the decade 1961–71. There is some evidence I think that the less skilled are remaining behind in the cities, whereas the jobs are beginning to migrate to the suburbs on the US pattern. Not only are the middle-level industrial jobs migrating very rapidly out of cities, but also many of the unskilled service jobs which these people could do are disappearing too. This is partly because the local, residentially based demand for services is migrating to the suburbs – that's obvious – but partly also because the new basic industries, above all tourism, also tend to migrate to suburbs. You now see Britain following the US pattern, with Holiday Inns developing at every interchange along the motorways. It means so many unskilled service jobs migrating out of the cities where the labour force for such jobs is still concentrated.

I think we have to consider the problem of how to ensure a more rapid migration of the unskilled out of the cities and into the suburbs. This has never been a popular policy. It has, of course, been systematically blocked in North America, where it is one of the major urban geographical problems. It has never occurred on a very widespread scale in this country. David Eversley has already noted that our much vaunted new towns policy has had very little success in getting unskilled people out of the cities. These people have remained behind, whereas the skilled and the semi-skilled have gone to the new towns, because these towns were too heavily based on factory jobs.

I think we have to find a way therefore of balancing the job demand and the supply of skill (or lack of skill) in the different parts of our growing metropolitan regions. Otherwise, either we shall have a tremendous problem of moving relatively unskilled people with low incomes and very poor access out of the centres of our cities to the suburbs every morning (the reverse commuting phenomenon which is now so common in American cities) or we shall find massive unemployment in the centres of the cities on the American model, with 20–25 per cent unemployment rates amongst certain groups in the central cities. (Such rates have subsequently been discovered for teenage coloured workers in parts of inner London. See G. Lomas, *The Inner City*, London Council of Social Service, 1975, p. 18.) This I think is the essential bundle of problems we are dealing with here and in order to achieve success we will need to look carefully at the role of the education system as well as our traditional planning policies. One aspect of a successful approach will be a much more careful questioning of what we can expect from schools in equipping people for a changing labour market and we will look at this issue in greater detail in Section Four.

2
The Government Response

We now begin our discussion of the different policies which combined to make Britain's urban programme. Dr Halsey recalls the birth of the Educational Priority Area programme (EPA). The need to discriminate positively by distributing educational resources in favour of poor children was one of the recommendations of the Plowden Report (HMSO, 1960). When the Report was presented to Anthony Crosland as Secretary of State for Education and Science, Michael Young (who had been a member of the Plowden Committee) was chairman of the SSRC and Chelly Halsey was part time adviser to the Minister. The Government sponsored the EPAs while the SSRC undertook to monitor the effect. This task was allocated to Dr Halsey.

1 The birth of educational priority areas *A. H. Halsey*

Harold Wilson took it into his head one Saturday afternoon in 1968 to declare a British urban crisis with £20 million to cure it. It was, I think, yet another example of ideas drifting casually across the Atlantic, soggy on arrival and of dubious utility. It gave us the community development programme.

Before that, in 1967, when Anthony Crosland was Secretary of State at the Department of Education and Science, I was his part-time adviser and Michael Young was chairman of the Social Science Research Council. We had received the Plowden Report. It belonged to native traditions of official proposals for class abatement but also had its transatlantic components, sent from Johnson's war on poverty and Coleman's survey of racial inequalities in education. It gave us the EPA action-research programme. If only for the sake of brevity, I want to assume that *Educational Priority: E.P.A. Problems and Policies*, vol. I, HMSO, 1972, may be taken as read.

(Vols II–V were also published by HMSO, in 1974 and 1975.)

Before that again, Derek Morrell at the Home Office had been nursing for several years his own version of a programme of community action and research. Morrell was a great man with a medieval mind, i.e. the sense of the eternity of wickedness, the need to build for ever and to overcome conflict by absorbing all interests into mammoth Gothic structures of organisation (the Schools Council was another of his cathedrals). He had little psychology and less sociology but he did have direct and daily access to the Deity (whom he tended to treat in the way that a powerful and determined permanent secretary treats his minister).

There was an organisational link between EPA and CDP in the early days of the latter. EPA started officially in the summer of 1968. The following summer Morrell asked me to take charge of the research side of the CDP. He was to have a full-time administrator (John Banks) and a full-time researcher (John Greve). We were at this stage in October 1969 when there was a Ditchley Conference with American Poverty War veterans. Then Morrell died and I withdrew into EPA, leaving Banks and Greve to carry on the development of the CDP programme.

There were thus some, but only some, things in common between the origins of EPA and CDP. Nevertheless, the differences of both organisation and conception were more important than the similarities. Some of them are of crucial significance for the underlying question as to what Gulbenkian might support. EPA, though sponsored by government and published by HMSO, has had a crucial degree of independence from officialdom which CDP has lacked. EPA also offers the example of a unitary organisation of action and research, whereas CDP is binary. These organisational differences have serious consequences, some of which are discussed in chapter 13 of *Educational Priority*, vol. I. A further set of implications are those which follow for policy formation when public enquiries are privately conducted. The relations between the EPA team, the civil servants and the politicians constitute a minor, but nevertheless fascinatingly instructive, case of the developing relations between government and social science in the processes of policy-making.

On the side of ideas I would emphasise that EPA was never conceived as a solution to a postulated 'urban crisis' and still less as a conception of urban conditions which had translated itself from the USA as a kind of British Koerner Report (accurately illuminating of US urban collapse into race riots and anarchy as that deadpan documentary undoubtedly was). I certainly, and my EPA colleagues probably, would lay no claim to comprehensive expertise on the problems of modern urbanism. Pretty much all we know is that US descriptions of the sub-working class, racial conflict, rootless males in matrifocal families, corrupt city government, etc., are to be treated as questions, not assumptions, in the making of urban policy in Britain.

Obviously, there is some version or another of a theory about community in current programmes. Obviously, too, there is some version or another of a theory about education as an agent of social change, and the conference must also dissect that. Our discussion will return to both points – to argue the need for a theory of community and the limitations of educational policy (pages 62 and 50). At this point I simply want to stress suspicion of Atlantic translations and my ignorance of the meaning to be attached to the phrase 'urban crisis'. Whose urban crisis? Crisis of what? Whatever the new answers, the questions are old. British sentimental traditions, popular and sophisticated, literary and social-scientific, are soaked in anti-urbanism. The 'crisis' of the industrial town was fussed over by nineteenth-century middle-class writers as the cradle of infectious disease, irreligion, physical squalor and political subversion. They, or rather the class whose fears they expressed, mostly escaped to suburbia in the twentieth century. The same 'crisis' was for the working class a challenge to social invention. They created the triple organisation of the Labour movement (the Party, the Unions and the Co-operatives) and the urban institutions which became in the process the way of life of the 'traditional' working class. Richard Hoggart (*The Uses of Literacy*, Chatto & Windus, 1958), Norman Dennis (*Coal is our Life*, Eyre & Spottiswoode, 1956), Young and Willmott (*Family and Kinship in East London*, Routledge & Kegan Paul, 1957) described them in the 1950s when some of them were already escaping either as Goldthorpe's affluent workers (J. H. Goldthorpe *et al.*, *The Affluent Worker*, Cambridge University Press, 3 vols, 1969) or as the people of the peripheral housing estates. See Peter Willmott, *The Evolution of a Community* and C. Rosser and C. Harris, *The Family and Social Change*, London, 1965. EPA and CDP are largely, though not wholly nor wholly properly, about what is left in the inner rings of the conurbations.

We lack an adequate sociological description of the inner rings now. It ought to be, or rather have been, the first major product of the CDP programme which began in 1969. Primarily from an educational point of view these areas of decay, shifting populations, bulldozers and redevelopment are pictured in chapters 4 and 5 of *Educational Priority*, vol. I. Two statements may suffice to recall the general flavour – a quarter of junior school children in the educational priority areas are virtually non-readers and the 'immigrants' are worse. Section 1 provided a fuller economic and social description. At all events, it is essential not to transpose American accounts of urban conditions without modification. This is not to say, however, that there are no similarities. For example, George Sternlieb's characterisation of 'The city as sandbox' (*The Public Interest*, no. 25, fall 1971, pp. 14–21) may be relevant. He claims that 'the major problem of the core areas of our cities is simply their lack of economic value' and goes on to argue that their new function is essentially that of a sandbox.

A sandbox is a place where adults park their children in order to converse, play or work with a minimum of interference. The adults, having found a distraction for the children, can get on with the serious things of life. There is some reward for the children in all this. The sandbox is given to them as their own turf. Occasionally, fresh sand or toys are put in the sandbox, along with an implicit admonition that these things are furnished to minimise the level of noise and nuisance. If the children do become noisy and distract their parents, fresh toys may be brought. If the occupants of the sandbox choose up sides and start bashing each other over the head, the adults will come running, smack the juniors more or less indiscriminately, calm things down and then, perhaps, in an act of semi-contrition, bring fresh sand and fresh toys, pat the occupants of the sandbox on the head, and disappear once again into their adult involvement and pursuits.

This is perhaps a description of the emerging relations of local government and the social services to districts labelled as EPA or CDP. (This metaphorical description has ominous affinities with Orwell's picture of the proletarian quarter in *1984*, being essentially a liberal version of the same phenomenon of disenfranchisement.)

After discussing the range of measures which make up the urban programme we turn to consider whether the programme is appropriately designed to tackle urban poverty. In the following contributions Frank Field argues that the basic assumption underlying the urban programme, that there are only small pockets of poverty, is very far from the truth. The contribution begins to develop an argument, which is taken up again in Chapter 4. This is that many, although not all, of the problems of the inner city would become much less serious if everyone was guaranteed an adequate income.

2 Britain's urban programme *Frank Field*

Successive governments have announced measures to tackle inner city poverty. As well as initiating educational priority areas (which are discussed by Dr Halsey in the last section), urban aid, community development projects (CDPs) and comprehensive community projects (CCPs) – section 11 grants, general improvement areas and housing action areas have also been devised to combat inner city poverty. In this section we examine the extent of the extra resources being devoted to deprived areas by each of these programmes.

Despite the evidence that Britain's urban crisis is not a racial one (see Alan Little's opening essay), the urban aid programme was initiated very shortly after Enoch Powell's 'rivers of blood' speech. The announcement was made by the Prime Minister on 5 May 1968, in Birmingham. During his speech Mr Wilson said: 'I am not prepared to stand aside and see this country engulfed by the racial conflict which calculating orators or ignorant prejudice can create' (*The Times*, 6 May 1968). Most of the press coverage was devoted to the Prime Minister's attack on racialism, both at home and in Rhodesia. *The Times'* leader in its comments on the urban aid programme dealt exclusively with the supposed worsening of race relations in Britain. However, immediately after Wilson's speech, politicians from all parties attempted to play down the fact that urban aid was initially concerned with lessening racial tensions, although no one has denied that areas gaining help are likely to be those with large numbers of immigrants.

From its inception, the urban aid programme has had only very limited resources at its disposal. In his statement outlining the programme, the Home Secretary informed the House of Commons that £20–25 million would be sanctioned over the next four years. In part, this limited budget stemmed from the government's continuing balance of payment difficulties, and in part because it appears that they believed that the scale of social provision was such that all but a few areas were already getting the resources needed. For example, Mr Callaghan, who was the first overlord of the programme, stated: 'The [government's] study shows that large and expanding programmes are already having an impact in each of the major social services concerned, and that in education and housing in particular, and in areas of immigrant settlement, priorities have been established within existing policies to increase the flow of aid to particular areas of special need.' The Home Secretary then went on to justify the establishment of the urban aid programme by saying: 'Nevertheless, there remain areas of serious social deprivation in a number of our cities and towns – often scattered in relatively small pockets. They require special help to meet their social needs, and to bring their physical services to an adequate level.' Overall, then, the programme was a topping-up operation which would ensure 'as far as we can, that all our citizens have an equal opportunity in life' (*Hansard*, 22 July 1968, vol. 769, col. 40–9).

In order that the programme could start at once, the first circular outlined a simple definition of social need. Areas would be eligible if they had either more than 2 per cent of households with more than $1\frac{1}{2}$ persons per room, or an exceptionally high immigrant population, i.e. more than 6 per cent of immigrants on the school roll. Initially, expenditure was limited to £2 million and went on the provision and expansion of nursery schools and classes, day nurseries and children's homes. Only 34 authorities were invited to apply for funds.

Since February 1969 the programme has expanded to cover all areas 'in which special social need is thought to exist'. Applications are received for projects establishing family and neighbourhood advice centres, teachers' centres, pre-school projects, family planning clinics, extra staff in housing departments, social centres for young people, English language and adaptation courses for immigrants, as well as the running of holiday projects. However, the hope expressed in the second circular, that in future the definition of special social need 'will be more highly developed', has not been fulfilled.

Two years after his first announcement, the Home Secretary stated that the programme, initially for four years, would be extended for a further four years, and that expenditure of up to £40 million would be authorised for the further period.

In July 1969 the Home Secretary announced the names of the first four local authorities who had agreed to take part in the community development project (CDP). He described the CDP as 'a radical experiment in community development involving local and central government, voluntary agencies and the universities in a concerted search for better solutions to deprivation than those we now possess . . . including the establishment of more valid and reliable criteria for allocating resources to the greatest social benefit' (Home Office Press statement, 16 July 1969).

In a paper which accompanied this announcement, it was stated that the CDP experiment was based on five assumptions. The first was that families suffering from chronic poverty or dependence on the social services tend to be found in large numbers in particular areas; for example, those suffering from urban and/or industrial decay.

Secondly, the experiment assumed that 'providing those families with more of the same form of social benefits and services, although helpful, will not be enough'. This assumption was closely allied to the third, which was that there are immobilised or untapped energies within communities, and that if these are successfully tapped a 'dramatic effect' can be expected. For example, many people would be released from their long-term dependence on the statutory social services. The fourth assumption underlying the CDP was that there was a great deal more need than was known to the official agencies, and that the gap between expressed and real need was partly caused by inadequate communication. The last assumption was based on the belief that we do not yet know the best ways of improving the living standards of poor communities.

The CDPs, therefore, share a common assumption with urban aid; nothing is so radically wrong with our society that a little topping-up of existing services (urban aid) or helping people gain access to them (CDPs) won't cure. With CDPs, the belief is that people's needs are met from a variety of different statutory and voluntary bodies, each generally failing to know of the others' existence, and of their respective relevance to the client. New kinds of activities by the projects aim at making services more accessible and comprehensible to those who might not otherwise see them as relevant to their needs. These activities will also aim to involve the people living in the area, but they will not cover the provision of facilities which are 'large, expensive, or wholly new in concept'. CDPs have, however, established new services – such as advice centres or pre-school groups – and these have been used as a means of making contact with local residents, finding out their grievances, and attempting to involve them in the project's work.

The effects of each CDP are being monitored. The researchers' job has not only been to help shape the project's activities, but to describe each stage in the development of the project and to provide the evidence of success or failure to the team as and when each monitoring exercise is complete. By the end of 1975 £62·4 million will have been spent on CDPs.

The intention to establish CCPs was announced in July 1974. In making the announcement, the government let it be known that it had decided on a new strategy for tackling urban deprivation, to be based upon the preparation by selected local authorities of CCPs for urban areas of the most acute deprivation. The 'essential purpose (of the CCP) is to bring about, through the co-ordinated efforts of central government, regional water and health authorities, local authorities, voluntary bodies and residents, a re-ordering of priorities in favour of those living in the most acutely deprived areas'. Initially, it is proposed to undertake a series of CCP 'trial runs' in four or five areas of England and Wales, and two in Scotland (Home Office press statement, 18 July 1974).

Few details have been made available of the kinds of programmes CCP will develop. It is thought that sums of around £1 million may be available to finance different experiments in each of the six or seven areas. If this proves to be true, then CCP may mark an important change in the development of the urban programme, for the CCP structure will allow experiments in improving the structure of the basic social welfare provision, albeit on a geographical basis. They will also be allowed to counter, in the smallest of ways, the problem of low wages, which is one of the root causes of poverty in the inner city. The need for attention to be focused in this direction is developed in the following section.

Two Government initiatives announced before the commencement of the urban aid scheme are now generally regarded as part of the urban programme. These are section 11 grants and general improvement areas (GIAs).

Section 11 of the Local Government Act 1966 empowers the Secretary of State to pay grants to local authorities in order to cover part of the cost of employing staff whose employment comes about as a consequence of the presence within the local area of substantial numbers of immigrants from the Commonwealth whose language and customs differ from the rest of the community. Authorities with 2 per cent or more Commonwealth immigrant pupils are considered as being *prima facie* eligible for grants. Where it can be shown that a local authority with less than 2 per cent Commonwealth immigrants on the school roll is incurring the sort of expense envisaged by section 11, then it too may be eligible for a grant.

Grants were originally paid at a rate of 50 per cent, but from 1 April 1969 this was increased to 75 per cent, the same rate as for urban programme expenditure. Section 11 grants are limited to the salaries and wages of relevant staff who are in the employ of the local authority. Claims have been made in respect of the salaries or wages of the following types of staff – liaison officers, interviewing staff and interpreters, clerical staff, teachers, ancillary helpers in schools, education welfare officers and social workers. By 1974–5 £43 million had been paid out in section 11 grants.

Public discussion has rightly centred on the poor quality of much of the housing stock in inner city areas. By the mid 1960s approximately 60,000–70,000 slums were being cleared a year (compared with an annual clearance rate of 90,000 slums in 1938). Improvement grants had been in existence since 1949 and by the 1960s were running at an annual rate of just over 100,000. This was considered too small a total and there was a growing concern that few of the worst houses were benefiting.

The 1969 Housing Act placed much greater emphasis on improving rather than replacing sub-standard housing. During the following two years the number of improvement grants allowed almost doubled. By 1973 over 360,000 grants were approved, but just as significant as the general rise is the increasing importance of discretionary grants – used to improve houses up to a prescribed standard, as opposed to standard and special grants – for the provision of basic amenities. Discretionary grants accounted for 40 per cent of all grants in 1968 and 88 per cent of grants in 1973.

The effect of the improvement policy on the quality of housing stock can be seen from the following information. In 1967 the number of unfit dwellings stood at 1·8 million. By 1971 this total had fallen to 1·2 million. Further, the number of additional dwellings that lacked one or more basic amenity stood at 2·3 million in 1967. By 1971 this total had fallen to 1·8 million. However, there is evidence to show that the improvement policy, while affecting the general level of housing provision, was not successful in making a radical impact on the housing of the poorest.

In order to remedy this failing the Heath administration introduced housing action areas (HAAs), which were taken up by the incoming Labour administration in 1974, to form a prominent part of the 1974 Housing Act. HAAs, together with priority neighbourhoods and GIAs, form the basis of the government's urban renewal strategy. They are intended to be a key item in the local authorities' armoury in the war against urban squalor. There are many similarities between HAAs and GIAs, but also certain specific differences. Unlike GIAs, HAAs are intended for use purely with private housing (whereas GIAs have also been extensively used to modernise council accommodation). In practice HAAs will have most relevance to inner city areas and, most particularly, inner London. Like GIAs, the size of HAAs will usually not exceed 200–300 houses. The intended characteristics and purposes of HAAs have been summarised in the circular DOE 13/7:

> HAAs should be areas of housing stress where bad physical and social conditions interact and where intense activity will immediately follow declaration. In HAAs, house renovation grants are payable at the highest rates, the conditions attached

to grants in respect of rented property are the most stringent, and the compulsory improvement provisions have been strengthened. Local authorities are given more specific powers to acquire property (by agreement or, where necessary, compulsorily), and have to be notified both of transactions in rented housing and of notices to quit.

By 31 October 1975 some 20,843 houses had come within HAA declarations (*Hansard*, 10 November 1975, vol. 899, col. 196).

Special action on inner city housing, the resources made available under section 11 grants, together with urban aid, CDP and CCP initiatives are the main policies underpinning Britain's urban programme. How successful it is in tackling inner city poverty is discussed in the next section but one.

3 The right urban programme? *Frank Field*

During the conference discussion Alan Little noted how small were the resources at the disposal of Britain's urban programme compared to the finances backing the attack on poverty in the USA. As we have seen from the previous contribution, the cost of the CDP and urban aid programmes between January 1968 and the end of 1976 will come to less than £80 million. In his oral contribution to the conference Alan Little went on to contrast this total with the estimates for the first year of the anti-poverty programme in the USA of $1 billion, and the criticism that was levelled at Congress when the Office of Economic Opportunity had its budget cut from $2·1 billion to $1·8 billion. He concluded by saying, 'In so far as willingness to mobilise resources is a measure of commitment to change, there can be little doubt about the relative seriousness of United States and United Kingdom efforts. For example the Community Relations Commission budget in the United Kingdom is currently around two-thirds of a million pounds. One project to assess the impact of negative income tax on minorities in the United States received twice as much.'

Despite the comparative smallness and limited range of Britain's urban programme we need to consider whether it is appropriate for combating urban poverty in this country. (Rural poverty is only just being rediscovered in Britain; see Marie Brown and Steve Winyard, *Low Pay on the Farm*, Low Pay Unit, 1975.)

The assumption underlying urban aid (see page 42) is that although there remain areas of serious social deprivation in a number of cities and towns these are confined to 'relatively small pockets'. How true is this basic assumption, which underlies the whole of the government's urban programme?

During the inter-war years, a number of poverty studies were carried out in various towns and cities around the country. These studies showed not only the number of people who were poor, but that many of the causes of poverty were identical to those found in Rowntree's first study in York in 1899. People became poor because they earned very low wages or were prevented from working through old age, sickness or unemployment. It was this poverty that the Beveridge reforms were supposed to abolish. National Insurance benefits, such as pensions and unemployment pay, were to be set at a level at or above the official poverty line. Those with sufficient contributions would therefore qualify for an income which would prevent them from becoming destitute. To combat family poverty caused by low wages, Beveridge proposed a generous system of family allowances, starting with the second child, and a system of free school dinners for every child.

We have a growing number of poor people today for two reasons. The first is that the Beveridge Report's proposals were never fully implemented. Insurance benefits are not paid at a high enough level. School dinners have never been free for every child, and family allowances have been prevented from becoming the meaningful additional source of income to the family which Beveridge had envisaged. Instead, more and more families qualify for means-tested assistance. Second, two new 'states of dependency', to use Richard Titmuss's words, have become recognised during the last thirty years; there has been a growth in the number of one-parent families, and of the sick and disabled. For most of the members of these two groups, there is no National Insurance coverage. The only form of help offered is means-tested supplementary benefits.

Supplementary benefits (which were first called National Assistance) were designed by Beveridge as a safety net which would gradually wither away as greater numbers earned their right to contributory National Insurance benefits. Because these benefits have never been paid at the value proposed by Beveridge, and because few people have enough savings to ensure a decent standard of living when they are unable to work, as well as the growth in new 'dependencies', an ever greater proportion of the population is forced to draw means-tested supplementary benefit in order to bring its income up to the state's poverty line.

Since 1948, when the national assistance scheme was introduced, the numbers drawing benefit have more than doubled. Today, nearly 5 million people's income and livelihood are dependent wholly or in part on means-tested supplementary benefits. This represents about 1 in 11 of the entire population.

An even greater number are dependent on means-tested rent rebates and allowances. Under the provisions of the Housing Finance Act, officials estimate that between 3 and 3·5 million heads of household (covering something like 12 million people) are unable to pay a 'fair rent' without suffering hardship. They are therefore eligible for means-tested assistance. Three million heads of household are also able to claim a means-tested rate rebate. Likewise, over a million children have parents who are unable to afford school dinners, and are therefore eligible for free school dinners. About 350,000 families claim free welfare food after submitting to a means test, and 140,000 family men who work earn such low wages that they are forced to supplement them with the means-tested Family Income Supplement.

The failure to implement fully the Beveridge plan, and to extend the scheme to one-parent families and the disabled, has resulted in an ever-growing army of people dependent on means-tested assistance. And as David Eversley showed, many of these people are to be found trapped in the inner city (see page 22). Trapped, because the new towns carefully select their inhabitants to exclude the low paid, unskilled, and those dependent on welfare. They are also caught in what has been called the 'poverty trap' (F. Field and D. Piachaud, 'The poverty trap', *New Statesman*, 3 December 1971): as income rises, the value of means-tested benefits falls, but the combination of both the loss of means-tested assistance and the low level of the tax threshold (the point where one begins to pay tax) results in a large number of families being made financially worse off as they try to improve their position. The response is, as Dr Eversley reminds us, either to conceal additional sources of income, or to fall into increasing apathy. Instead of acting as a floor on which people can seize initiatives and help build a better life for themselves, means-tested benefits form a ceiling, trapping the poor into their poverty.

This information, together with the evidence of the growing disparity between the living standards of the poorest and those enjoying an average standard of living, makes it difficult to accept the basic premise behind the urban aid programme – namely, that only small pockets of poverty remain. Poverty is widespread, and there is evidence to suggest that the gap between the very poor and the rest of the community is widening. Taking the very poorest and those on average earnings gives a different result from the analysis David Eversley quotes of the living standards of those in the upper and lower quartile of the income distribution (see page 19). Of course, the standard of living of the poorest is higher than that of the poor of pre-war Britain. But this should not blind us to the fact that we have a growing number of poor in the Britain of the 1970s, and the evidence suggests that they are disproportionately concentrated in inner city areas. The belief held by many politicians and the electorate alike, that poverty has been abolished by the welfare state, does not stand up to examination, and it is within this perspective that we have to view what is going on in the inner city.

When the conference began analysing the proposals for action contained in the Halsey Report, John Vaizey introduced the session by drawing attention to the dual strategy in the report. Some of the Halsey Report's recommendations were concerned with education itself, but others stressed the limitations of educational reforms and concentrated the attention of the conference on the need to reform the wider society.

4 The importance of the Halsey Report *John Vaizey*

We ought to be able to agree among ourselves that both technological progress and social action were capable of dealing with gross material deprivation. What the Halsey Report has to say to us at this particular time is that the problem of social deprivation in the conurbations has taken a particular form to which we have not yet devised relevant solutions which have been widely adopted. The solution that Halsey is proposing seems to fall into two parts. The first part is that it requires positive and coherent action by all sorts of bodies – public and private – in the field of employment, housing and education for any one of these things to succeed. And secondly, specifically in the field of education, it is necessary for the school in the areas of tension to take a much more outgoing role than it has previously done. That is to say that the older idea – like the grammar school, which was a school closed in on itself where boys and girls arrived very early in the morning and stayed until late at night in order to escape, as Lawrence did to Nottingham University – is the reverse of the kind of school that we ought to be thinking of for the great majority of children in the inner cities. It is these two lessons which seem to be spelt out explicitly in the Halsey Report and which I take as the basic issues we have to discuss.

In an earlier contribution Dr Halsey agreed that it is necessary for the conference to discuss the limits placed on educational reform in trying to achieve equality in education. Stephen Jessel takes up this issue by reviewing the relevant portion of the Halsey Report. The following sections also summarise the main recommendations of the Report. In doing so our discussion begins to focus on a viable programme of educational and social reform which is developed in Chapter 4.

5 What did Halsey propose? *Stephen Jessel*

In October 1972 the first of five volumes describing a project designed to improve the educational experiences of children from poor homes in deprived areas was published. Entitled *Educational Priority*, it was mostly the work of Dr A. H. Halsey, national director of the project, which had been commissioned by the Department of Education and Science and the Social Science Research Council at a cost of £175,000.

The project and the subsequent report had their origins in the discussions that followed the 1967 Plowden Report on children and their primary schools. Two of the recurring themes of Plowden were the need to discriminate positively in favour of some children and the need for 'action research'. This new, and not always easy, concept is defined at its simplest as small-scale interventions in the functioning of the real world, usually in administrative systems, and the close examination of the effects of such interventions.

Eventually five teams were established in Educational Priority Areas (EPAs). These were in the Deptford area of London, in Liverpool, in the Balsall Heath district of Birmingham, in the West Riding of Yorkshire, and in Dundee. The aim of these teams was to explore and experiment with practical means of raising educational standards in these deprived areas.

In the first volume devoted to the experiences of the EPAs Dr Halsey gives a general account of the studies and their findings in the English EPAs, together with various recommendations for policy. Since the EPA teams were only funded for three years, the report was written after all but a little of the work had been completed.

' "To find a strategy for educational roads to equality." That has been a central theme of educational discussion from the beginning of the twentieth century.' These are the first two sentences of the Halsey Report and they indicate the theme of the first third of the report, which draws in the background to a continuing debate about equality in education, and interprets that debate in the light of the significance of positive discrimination and the content of the education needed by children in EPAs.

The opening chapter traces theories of compensatory education and discusses the interrelationships of efficiency, equality and justice. The essential fact of contemporary egalitarian policies is that they have failed, the report says, as it delineates the form of the developing debate about the way education can be used as a means towards the political and social end of equality.

The initial failure, it suggests, is basically attributable to a failure to notice that the major determinants of educational achievement are 'not schoolmasters but social situations, not curriculum but motivation, not formal access to the school but support in the family and the community'. So that brand of social philosophy was succeeded by a shift of emphasis towards a greater concentration on blending social and educational opportunity. Equality of opportunity, in short, without equality of conditions is a sham; and that is the conclusion of the Plowden Report.

But even this second stage begs certain questions. What is education for? 'The debate over equality . . . is essentially a discussion about education for whom and to do what. In planning our intervention in schools we were forced sooner or later to consider whether an EPA programme is anything more than a new formula for fair competition in the educational selection race.'

And that, of course, raises a whole army of questions, particularly in so far as the curriculum is concerned. On one side Halsey identifies the Plowden thesis that schools in backward areas should be brought up to scratch so that the children from them should leave as well equipped to compete as those from better-favoured areas. On the other hand is what one might term the Midwinter approach, that part of the basic trouble is the existence of determined values, a consensus approach. What was needed was a variety of goals to correspond to a variety of circumstances.

Halsey examines various theories of poverty, both as identified in Britain and as identified in the United States. He concludes that the poverties to which urban industrial populations are prone must be understood to have their origins in both situational and cultural characteristics of those minorities which suffer disadvantage and discrimination, and to have the cures in both economic and cultural reform, not only at the local or community level but also in the total structure of society.

The varied (but on the whole disappointing) experience of compensatory education in the USA is reviewed at some length. In brief, the US programmes began with what seemed to be a simple educational problem; namely, that certain social groups on average had a lower level of educational performance. In the effort to solve this problem the researchers found themselves forced to go further and further away from purely educational grounds as the extent of the whole problem became evident.

'In this process the most basic questions are raised about the nature of social organisation and about the reasons why lower social status should be associated with lower educational performance. These developments indicate that a purely educational response to the initial problem is unlikely to succeed.'

Educational under-achievement has become only one manifestation of a series of social and economic disparities experienced by disadvantaged groups, and the long-term solution must be a comprehensive policy which strikes at these economic inequalities.

How did the government react to the Plowden Report? The designation of the EPAs and the acceptance of the principle of 'positive discrimination' were the most obvious responses. Halsey describes how the professional organisations reacted to these steps and the political and financial measures which were taken to implement the report's recommendations. Teachers in EPA schools were paid an extra £75 a year, later raised to £83, though the committee had suggested £120. Nothing much more was heard of the plan to introduce teachers' aides in the priority schools in a ratio of one to every two junior and infant classes.

In general, efforts to turn the idea of a priority school into a reality and to devise ways of following up the recommendations of Plowden have derived largely from the enthusiasm and commitment of a small group of people. Local experience has undoubtedly opened up a great range of possibilities and the urban aid programme has allowed some significant advances. The question now, says Halsey, is whether the government is prepared to launch a full-scale national policy.

The report then goes on to describe and discuss the experience of the researchers in the EPAs. The question of what constitutes an EPA, the amount of provision of pre-schooling, the various experiments in pre-schooling, and the relationship between the community school on the one hand and, in turn, the family, the curriculum, the teachers and the wider community on the other hand, are reviewed in the second section of the report.

An examination of the four English Plowden EPAs concludes that while they all undoubtedly suffer from multiple economic and social deprivation, and the schools within them suffer from the difficulties brought into them by the nature of the neighbourhood, there is nevertheless no unique single feature that distinguishes the EPA or the EPA school. What is true of the West Riding is not necessarily true of the Liverpool or Deptford area, and what is true of either of those is not necessarily true of Balsall Heath.

Reviewing existing provision in the areas, Halsey comments that the research teams became aware of the need not just for expansion but for types of provision which would maximise the effectiveness of positive discrimination and lay the foundations for radical improvement of the partnership between the organised state system and the community. The teams were particularly impressed by the potential contribution, and until then largely neglected use, of the reserves of energy and enthusiasm among the parents of pre-school children in EPA districts.

A largely technical chapter, much of it devoted to the experience of groups which have used US material to develop the language of children, suggests that children in EPA areas who follow a properly constructed programme make greater strides in language than those who do not; but the evidence is not compelling. Other experiments have been slightly more conclusive. In the West Riding (some would regard this as one of the most important findings of the whole EPA experiment) initial gains were retained in the infant school. Work in Birmingham showed that the acquisition of concepts of number could be speeded up. Experience in London highlighted the need for teachers' classroom behaviour to be guided to promote the development of children; from Liverpool came the message that pre-schooling needs to use locally oriented materials and methods.

The report discusses the involvement of parents. 'It must be a significant advance if schools could be encouraged to run child–parent projects attempting to make sure that every parent has at least one chance of such an experience during the child's time at school.'

Curriculum development is also reviewed, and the controversial conclusions of the Liverpool team are outlined. These are that there should be a shift from academic to social emphasis, in the sense that the children's activities should be rooted more deeply in their own experience; that the balance should shift further towards creative pursuits; that skills rather than information should be a theme of social environmental studies; and that 'teaching attitudes and the atmosphere of the school must change. EPA community education presumes that the EPA should be radically reformed and the children should be "forewarned and forearmed for the struggle".'

As for the community school – a key concept in EPA philosophy – and its relationship to the community, Halsey agrees that there can be no easy answers. Community schools in working-class areas have often failed because the people in charge of them have gone for a narrow, formal and traditional approach. The community side has often been nothing more than the ordinary further education centre attached to the existing buildings.

'The community school must be prepared to listen to parents, to advise and assist, rather than tell "them" what "we" think they should do. Community and social workers have learnt this lesson and adult educationists must do likewise. This is no easy task. It may mean a new type of professional, a community adult educationist attached to community schools.'

Halsey devotes an entire chapter to an explanation and critique of action-research, arguing that it brings together two professions, social science and administration, which have traditionally kept apart and developed their own methods. He distinguishes several possible uses of the term, and identifies five broad contexts in which it can be used. He tries to place the EPA experiment in its correct category and concludes by examining the implications for research of the practice of action-research.

> The traditional separation of action and research as separate activities with their own ideologies is in part responsible for the confusion over the nature of action-research. Obviously there is no automatic identity of interest between the two spheres, though it may be that the differences have been over-emphasised. There has been a tendency to see facts and values as different social objects with different procedures of investigation necessary to each one. This approach cannot be sustained; social science which is to be significant must be value-based. It cannot be a value-free collection of facts. The action-research contest exposes this truth – perhaps unpleasantly.

Action-research is unlikely ever to yield neat and definite prescriptions from field-tested plans. 'What it offers is aid to intelligent decision-making, not a substitute for it. Research brings relevant information rather than uniquely exclusive conclusions.'

But it does prompt recommendations. In the final part of his report Halsey offers seven such proposals.

1. The educational priority area, despite difficulties of definition, is a socially and administratively viable unit through which to apply the principle of positive discrimination.

The problem of deciding just what constitutes an EPA is acknowledged. Local authorities have no common formula for identifying what makes an educational priority area. Halsey suggests that three points should be borne in mind. First, measures of pupil and teacher turnover taken from schools may be useful indicators of the multiple problems of areas; and measures of language difficulty are neither conterminous with immigrants as officially defined nor accurately reflected in school records (a point amply borne out by the report of the Select Committee on immigrants' education). Second, urban decay is not limited to the centres of the big conurbations. Overcrowding, high numbers of immigrants, and multi-occupancies are not the only criteria that should be used; economic prospects should also be taken into account. We ought to look more closely at groups forced to leave small towns by industrial and economic change to see whether their displacement from one area does not in fact lead to increased overcrowding and social pressures in others, perhaps the centres of the large cities where they may end up in search of employment.

The third point to be remembered is that in the end the appropriate unit for positive discrimination is the individual and the family. The district is no more than a device, and not a perfectly accurate device, for identifying an area of problem within which the closer and more detailed work has to be done through schools, school classes, individuals and families if a fully effective policy of positive discrimination is to be developed. The report recommends the retention of the geographical definition and its widening to include a greater number of schools than the present list. The criteria of definition should be flexible enough to embrace a wider variety of multiply deprived districts; not just in city centres, but in economically declining urban areas, in redevelopment housing estates and in some rural areas.

2. Pre-schooling is the outstandingly economical and effective device in the general approach to raising standards in the EPAs. Three conclusions were reached by the researchers. Pre-schooling was *par excellence* a point of entry into the development of the community school. Primary and secondary attainment rests on the social foundations of the child's experience. There is no unique blueprint of either organisation or content. For those reasons some possible policies can be eliminated, one such being the introduction of a nationally standardised starting age for school of four. The report largely dismisses formal nursery education, arguing that the home is the key educational influence, and that formal pre-schooling is of marginal importance and cannot be compensatory in the sense that it substitutes educational influences lacking in the home.

'We advocate a hybrid form of nursery centre which is neither the expensive professionally run nursery school nor the cheap and parent-run but amateur playgroup. The hybrid may be expected to inherit the vigour of both stocks. It is focused on learning, and therefore needs professional guidance, a carefully worked out curriculum and organised links with the infant school, but at the same time it needs parental co-operation and community involvement.' Halsey reviews some of the experiments tried in the EPAs in this field, arguing the importance of a partnership between voluntary and statutory interests in the organisation of his proposed hybrid. On the question of content, he draws attention to the findings of the West Riding experiment, in which it was found that children receiving pre-schooling retained their gains in the first year of the infant school. (The significance of this being that it runs counter to the US experience which is widely cited as an argument against the introduction of pre-schooling on any large scale.)

3. The idea of the community school, as put forward in skeletal outline in the Plowden Report, has now been shown to have greater substance and powerful implications for community regeneration. Halsey sees the concept of the community school as an essential principle, together with that of positive discrimination, in any EPA policy. 'The community school seeks almost to obliterate the boundary between school and community, to turn the community into a school and the school into a community. It emphasises both teaching and learning roles for all social positions so that children may teach and teachers learn as well as vice versa, and parents may do both instead of neither.'

Halsey is not sentimental about the community school and recognises the ambiguity of the word 'community' in this context; a Yorkshire mining village is a community in a different sense of the word from the inner city slum. The community school has to be more than a device for co-ordinating and concentrating separate educative forces; it has also to be pervaded by a relevant conception of the curriculum needed for the education of children in EPAs, which in turn depends upon standards of teaching. He also recognises the difficulties of governance and management.

4. From the idea of the community school flows the observation that there are practical ways of improving the partnership between school and family. That means improving the image of education in the eyes of parents. It entails exposition of what the scheme is trying to do – improve the local environment. Halsey suggests a public relations grant of £150 a school or 50p a head. Education has to be taken to the home and the home to the school, with the 'educational visitor' playing an important part, as should the home–school liaison teacher. Parents must be encouraged to understand the process through which their children are being educated.

5. There are practical ways of improving the quality of teaching. These have to be carried out on several levels, in terms of motivating, equipping and supporting teachers on their side of the partnership. Teachers have to be given smaller classes, proper curriculum materials, teachers' aides, teachers' centres, effective links with colleges of education and other sources of relevant information. Extra payments should mark the superior professional challenge of teaching in difficult schools, not be regarded as 'dirt money'. Both the curriculum and teaching attitudes need to change. In the former case it must be rooted in the child's own experience, while full attention is devoted to the basic importance of language and emphasis laid on the development of skills rather than the assimilation of information. For their part teachers must become less identified with the forces of the status quo and more sympathetic to the moral and social climate in which the children they teach are growing up. Halsey does not underestimate the hurdle presented by the need to direct teaching virtues to a compassionate, tolerant and critical examination of all social, political and moral issues on the way towards a community-oriented curriculum. 'It could take years and it will require a generous and sympathetic change of heart, not only among educational authorities but in society at large.'

6. Action-research is an effective method of policy formulation and practical innovation. The report restates its belief in action-research, and claims success in the fields of discovery and innovation, while accepting the need for further research. But dissemination of the discoveries and innovations of action-research needs a different agency. The report suggests that a team of six or seven could channel materials and funds, establish networks of action and communication and create the essential impetus for change and innovation. They could act semi-independently within the framework of large local education authorities or consortia of similar authorities.

7. The EPA can be no more than a part, albeit an important part, of a comprehensive social movement towards community development and redevelopment in a modern industrial society. Any educational approach to poverty and deprivation has its limits. But within these limits there can be seen a viable road to a higher educational standard of living for hundreds and thousands of children in the more disadvantaged districts.

'We would hope that there is sufficient confidence in our results from the first projects for the government and the local education authorities to create the framework of organisation for pre-schooling and community schooling that we have advocated. If so there will be a new landmark in British educational progress.'

What has been the government's response to the EPAs programme? In the following section Dr Halsey reviews the limited but nevertheless important influence the report has had on both the Heath Administration's education plans as well as those of the third and fourth Wilson governments. But these reforms will not automatically be to the complete advantage of families and children. Dr Halsey expresses a concern that they may weaken the ties between parents and children and see a further strengthening of bureaucratic and professional control over the lives of individuals. In order to resist these two trends Dr Halsey begins to develop his ideas about community and the limitation of educational reform alone in bringing about a more equal society.

6 The governmental response to EPAs *A. H. Halsey*

The Oxford EPA programme was a three-year cycle of action-research. It was conceived in Curzon Street, born in Oxford, brought up in Deptford, Birmingham, Liverpool, the West Riding and Dundee, and finally returned as a mature set of findings and recommendations to Mrs Thatcher at the DES. The message carried by it had five parts.

1. An educational policy for the educational priority areas.
2. Established EPA practices in the experimental areas.
3. An action organisation – Priority – based in Liverpool but national in scope.
4. A research organisation – the social evaluation unit in the Department of Social and Administrative Studies at Oxford, and
5. Proposals for further research and action-research in EPAs.

And meanwhile, it should be added that further educational priority action-research had been built into several of the CDP projects.

The policy is set out in chapter 14 of *Educational Priority*, vol. I, and had its reflections in the Conservative government's White Paper on *Education: a Framework for Expansion* (Cmnd 5174, HMSO, 1972). These reflections were welcome but they were vague, muted and partial. We called for a particular type of pre-school programme and the government promised a Plowden level of provision. But the schedule was a slow one. The Plowden targets were not to be reached until 1981 and the sums made immediately available were extremely modest. We asked for positive discrimination and 'Priority will be given in the early stages of the programme to areas of disadvantage'. This was far too vague. It ought to have been written in terms of precise measurement and as an explicit financial formula. There was a hopeful reference to the experience of the urban programme, which uses the techniques of phasing and further grant aid only after inspection. But again, a positively discriminatory programme needs to have close central control. It is dangerous to leave too much to local councils. Of course we want local diagnosis before plans are made for pre-school provision, but within the framework of firm central criteria for grant aid and a strong central organisation to ensure that the pre-school resources flow to those who are most in need of them. This will not happen unless the DES sets up a division concerned with what is, after all, a new stage of education and does so with firm inter-departmental arrangements with the Department of Health and Social Security. In 1975, crisis having succeeded crisis, we still wait for these administrative developments. And as for finance, the prospects for 1976 and 1977, under the present Labour government, appear to put even the Plowden 1981 targets in jeopardy.

We wanted local diagnosis and avoidance of standard national formulae as to the organisation and curricula of nursery education and 'The government attached importance to a full assessment of local resources and needs, and would welcome diversity'. We advocated the hybrid vigour of professional nurseries and parent-involved playgroups, and the government promised to guide and encourage local authorities to equip voluntary groups and provide them with qualified teachers, recognising that 'the maturity and experience (of mothers) are important assets' and that 'nursery education probably offers the best opportunities for enlisting parental understanding and support for what schools are trying to achieve'. These clearly were reflections of our chapter 14 and the discussions we had with Mrs Thatcher and the civil servants in the DES. In the White Paper, however, Mrs Thatcher seems to have defined need in terms of parental wishes – a recipe for negative discrimination or the well-known process of skimming. And again, diagnosis could easily and fatally be left to unguided and unaided local government interests. The educational anthropology which we advocated as the basis for deciding on forms of provision requires task forces to work with the local interests, both statutory and voluntary, and both educational and social services.

Moreover, the last quotation from the White Paper was a very partial reflection indeed of the idea of community schooling which has otherwise been entirely neglected by the government, whereas for us it is the essential concept, along with positive discrimination, in any educational contribution to the raising of standards of life in EPA or CDP districts.

The other four parts of our message to the DES still belong mainly to the future. The continuing EPA action in London, Birmingham, Liverpool, the West Riding and Dundee would well repay an evaluative re-visit next year or the year after. At the West Riding Red House there is, in any case, an action-research programme still under way financed by the SSRC. We are also studying the impact of nursery school expansion on private provision and need in Birmingham. *Priority* has had a large influence under Eric Midwinter's energetic leadership. The Social Evaluation Unit in Oxford is active in monitoring two of the CDP projects in Liverpool and Birmingham, though CDP may also soon fall victim to cuts in public expenditure.

As to our proposals for further research, there was an encouraging note in the White Paper. But little has come of it, despite the return of a Labour government. The SSRC organised a seminar, ably launched by Barbara Tizard's review of *Pre-School Education in Great Britain* at the end of 1974 – a book edited by Barbara Tizard on this seminar was published in 1975 – and afterwards gave a large grant for further research under the direction of Professor Jerome Bruner at Oxford. Mrs Thatcher's successor as Secretary of State under the new Labour administration was Reg Prentice. He held a conference on educational deprivation in April 1975 at which the establishment of a unit in the DES concerned with educational deprivation was publicised and a Centre for Dissemination at Manchester, under the chairmanship of Sir Alec Clegg, was announced. It began operation in the autumn of 1975 and acts as an information centre independent of the DES concerned with giving advice on curriculum, teaching methods, etc. and on good practice generally relevant to the education of the disadvantaged and immigrants. Both these developments presumably owe something to our 1971 proposals.

The Thatcher White Paper gave us a clear promise that some kind of nursery system of education will be nationalised in the next decade. Nevertheless, the main body of our recommendations awaits realisation in the future. On present promises it could turn out to be a very different future from the one I want. My desire, perhaps romantic and perhaps falsely nostalgic if not reactionary, is for a pluralistic society, an equal distribution of power and advantage, strong and stable families, and a welfare-providing community which, from the point of view of the growing individual, enlarges its scope at each successive stage of education, work and leisure. Thus, for example, though I welcome the government's intentions towards a nursery stage of education, I fear a further weakening of the ties

between parents and children and a further strengthening of bureaucratic and professional control of the lives of individuals if the forms
of nursery schooling do not rest on a triangular conception of
teachers, parents and children exchanging both teaching and
learning on each of the three sides. Nursery education could be a
further step towards the domination of the family by administrative
organisations rather than towards a more effective partnership
between the two great educative forces of kin and school. Similarly,
our proposal for an educational visitor service could serve, in the
end, either to support the family or to subjugate it.

But the key words in this summary conception of a future society
are 'community' and 'equality'. Thus we are brought back to the
references I made earlier (page 40) concerning the need for a theory
of community and a realistic appraisal of the role of education in
social change. Taken together, our EPA recommendations are
intended as a contribution to both. The details need not be re-
hearsed. It is, however, worth repeating that educational reform
has not brought in the past and is unlikely in the future ever to bring
an egalitarian society unaided. An EPA policy in effect assumes
fundamental reforms in the economic and social institutions which,
by and large, it can only reflect. Given these reforms – which include
the devolution of power to localities; democratic control by community members over national and professional purveyors of
expertise in planning, health, employment and education; income
and capital equalisation; co-ordinated employment policies and well-
planned housing and civic amenities – then realistic demands can be
put on the education system. The schools can be asked, in partnership with the families they serve, to bring up children capable of
exercising their political, economic and social rights and duties in
such a society. They can, of course, be so constituted as to socialise
children in anticipation of such a society: but to do so without the
wider reforms is to court frustration for individuals if not disaster
for the social order.

The idea of community in such a society is no simple one. For the
pre-school and primary school child it can have a fairly straightforward geographical meaning – a bounded territory within which
the individual can satisfy his human needs. But even at this level
the need to plan for stabilities – for example, in housing and employment of families, in the continuity of service by teachers to classes
and in the regularity of civic and social services, is of the utmost
importance. But the meaning of community goes beyond the constraints of a known and reliable territory. It has the deeper meaning
of shared values which are reinforced time after time in daily

encounters in the home, on the street, in the school and in the public institutions. The sharing of values pre-supposes consensus on an ordered set of criteria of human relations. In a society like ours, these values must be a combination of the equalities which may be derived from justice, the recompense which is due to arbitrary misfortune and at the same time a recognition and tolerance of a wide range of life styles, whether they come from differences of racial and cultural origin or from the choices made available in a society which is economically rich. Equality and liberty so defined need subtle reconciliation and thus immensely challenge the capacities of those who dare to undertake social planning. Yet that combination must be the meaning which we seek to give to the word 'community'.

3
What is happening in Inner City Schools?

In this section we piece together evidence on what is happening in inner city schools. Alan Little begins our discussion by asking whether developments in inner city schools are products of changes within the schools themselves, or if the answer is to be found elsewhere. He quotes evidence to show that educational standards in many urban schools are declining. There is some evidence to suggest that there is a greater proportion of 'maladjusted' children in inner city schools than elsewhere. However, he goes on to show that some of the problems of the urban school are the product of earlier maturation and the changing attitude to authority, and that both these changes are having effects throughout the education system.

1 Declining pupil performance and the urban environment
Alan N. Little

As far as schools situated in inner city areas are concerned, there have been many studies of school performance. A recent example is an attempt of Barnes, in which he compared backward readers in primary schools throughout the equivalent of the ILEA in 1952/54 with 1968/71 and more limited comparisons in the area within which an EPA study took place. In 1953 the LCC took a sample of schools from which they derived a representative sample of children; of this sample 14 per cent of the 11-year-olds were described as backward (using the criterion of a reading score below 85). In 1968 a cohort of 8-year-olds contained 27 per cent with a reading score of 85 and below and the same cohort three years later yielded a similar percentage. Assuming a normal distribution the expected proportion scoring below 85 is 16 per cent. Therefore, it is possible to argue that in the early 1950s LCC primary school leavers were performing at a marginally higher level than expected and that by 1968 they were doing significantly worse than the national average. At this point it is worth noting that the mean score of all ILEA pupils aged 8 in 1968 was 94·4 (equivalent to a 6-month retardation in reading age) and at 11 94·2 (equivalent to a 10-month retardation in reading age). The important observation is that in the early 1950s roughly one pupil in seven was defined as being backward: by 1968/71 one pupil in four or nearly twice as many could be categorised as backward.

These figures relate to reading and to primary schools, but a wealth of information exists to show a high correlation between reading and other skills taught in primary schools and between primary and secondary school performance. Therefore reading can be taken as a fair indication of basic skill performance. Given this a further point can be made using reading scores; the ILEA developed an index of educational priority areas (i.e. socially disadvantaged), based upon the type of criteria suggested by Plowden. A recent study has related reading scores to EPA rank of the school. When schools were divided into quartiles, the mean reading score of pupils in the least privileged quartile was 89·2, compared with 100·4 in the most privileged quartile. Translated into reading ages this means that pupils in the beginning of the second year of junior school in the most privileged areas had a mean reading score well over a year above their age peers in the least privileged areas. It also means that inner city areas contain a variety of schools which can be differentiated in terms of pupil performance.

Concern about behavioural standards covers a wide canvas. For some it relates to specific behaviour like truancy, delinquent behaviour, vandalism and violence within the school. Most of this is anecdotal and impressionistic (as are the contributions which follow at the end of this section), but it certainly gives a picture of the inner city school being more difficult to teach and learn in than the outer city counterpart. Undoubtedly some of the descriptions of what is going on and, perhaps more important, predictions of what will happen, derive from looking at the current UK situation through a series of preconceptions derived from experiences within the USA and therefore of questionable usefulness in the UK context.

Nevertheless, concern about the prevalence of maladjustment in city schools is confirmed by the work of Rutter and others. Rutter has developed a scale of pupil maladjustment based on teacher ratings of individual pupils. An extreme comparison is instructive for the purpose of our debate. Using Rutter's own operational definition of maladjustment the percentage of pupils rated as maladjusted in the Isle of Wight was 10·6 per cent. By contrast, the percentage in primary schools in an inner city borough in the ILEA at the same time was 19·1 per cent. As a result of this finding a special survey was undertaken of one in ten pupils aged 11-plus in the ILEA: these were scored by their classroom teacher on the Rutter scale. This indicated that 21·6 per cent were maladjusted. It seems safe to conclude that the incidence of 'maladjustment' is twice as high in inner city areas as in small towns in Britain. In this context it is worth noting that the reading scores of maladjusted pupils were of considerable educational interest: whereas the mean for pupils classified as normal was 96·6, those considered to be maladjusted had a mean score over ten points lower (86·2). Put another way, whereas 'good readers' had a mean behaviour rating of 2·3, for poor readers the comparable figure was 7·6. Therefore the inner city school is likely to have more maladjusted pupils and they are more likely to be poor performers in school. This point about relative performance of pupils 'at risk' is worth making in relation to social disadvantage. Again, to cite literacy data and the EPA index: pupils were ranked according to the level of their own exposure to social disadvantages and grouped into low-risk (no disadvantage) and high-risk (exposed to five or more disadvantages). The mean reading score of pupils with no disadvantage was 103·8; with five or more disadvantages 81·5. This is a gap of more than 22 points and is the equivalent of more than two years' reading age at 8 or 9. Put simply: disadvantaged children do less well than advantaged, and inner city schools have more disadvantaged children than other schools. Maladjusted children do less well than adjusted and inner city schools have more maladjusted children than other schools. The dynamics of this relationship are analysed in a recent study in the ILEA (and quoted by Frank Field in the introductory essay) which indicates that 'educational failure' precedes and gives rise to behavioural difficulties, rather than the other way round. Further, that other factors (class, family size, immigrant status) which are related to maladjustment 'do so to a considerable extent only through their effects on academic perform-ance'. On this analysis social factors cause poor performance, which in turn may generate maladjustment: further, regardless of social factors, poor educational performance is seen as a cause rather than a consequence of maladjustment. However, this behaviour is not peculiar to the inner city schools: it is the high incidence that is.

Concern about teachers and teaching is made up of three separate points: the difficulty of recruiting teachers in inner city schools;

the difficulty of retaining teachers in inner city schools; the difficulty of recruiting/retaining experienced teachers. The scale of the recruitment problem facing a large urban education authority is illustrated by a study completed five years ago in the ILEA. The size of the teaching force was under 20,000, and in a single year 4,775 teachers resigned from the authority's service; this is 23·8 per cent of the stock. The broad magnitude of teaching turnover has been confirmed by a DES enquiry in 1972/73. Amongst primary school teachers in the ILEA, the overall turnover level was 33·4 per cent of the stock and in secondary schools 25·9 per cent. Nevertheless, the turnover for all LEAs was 17·6 per cent and 15·3 per cent respectively.

Therefore, an authority like the ILEA has nearly twice as high a turnover rate as the rest of the country, and is confronted by the problem of recruiting 5,000 teachers every year. The difficulty facing individual schools in retaining experienced teachers is well illustrated by an earlier ILEA survey: of the permanent teachers who resigned, 77 per cent of the men and 87 per cent of the women had been teaching in their last school for less than five years. Inevitably, individual schools (and especially primary schools) are faced with the joint problem of high staff turnover and few teachers with more than a limited amount of teaching experience. Again, the ILEA index of educational priority areas is relevant. One of the criteria was a measure of teacher turnover; namely the percentage of teachers who had been in the school for less than three years. National data suggested that the average figure should be about 25 per cent: in the school ranked first (i.e. most disadvantaged in terms of the index) three-quarters of the staff had been at the school for less than one year. In the school ranked 50th the proportion was two-thirds, and in the school ranked 100th it was nearly half. (How the cutbacks in public expenditure, which are resulting in a growing problem of unemployment amongst teachers, are affecting this situation is considered in the following essay, see page 125.)

There is no doubt that a case can be made advocating the special needs for inner city schools. However, we ought to be considering a further set of questions: how far the difficulties facing the inner city school are the result of the character of the inner city area and how far they are the product of more general changes throughout society and the educational system. Three general changes are worth examining in this context: the effect of earlier maturation; changes in authority relationships; modification of educational objectives and practices. The common element of these points is to suggest that the concerns people have about inner city schools are in part the result not of changes within the city but of the sort of factors outlined above. That pupils are maturing earlier is accepted: for example the age of menarche has been reduced by nearly a year in a generation. Young people of both sexes are maturing physically far quicker than previous generations, allied to which certain aspects of psychological and social development have also accelerated. Much behaviour (both socially approved and disapproved) once associated with late adolescence and early adulthood is now common amongst early and mid-adolescents. It is tempting to illustrate this with behaviour that is frequently disapproved of (smoking, drinking, sexual experimentation, etc.). Equally relevant is behaviour (ranging from political participation to sophistication in styles of dress and other patterns of consumption) to which the adult generation reacts in a more neutral and approving manner.

Allied to this, changes in authority relationships generally may well have influenced the relationship between pupil and teacher. Traditionally both age and class hierarchies were clearly established and widely accepted. Children deferred to their elders (especially parents) and social deference (working-class towards middle-class) was commonplace. A variety of macrosocial changes have at least modified these relationships. The cult of youth among both adolescents and adults implies a change in the relationship between age hierarchies, and the frequent demonstration of changing income differential between certain grades of manual and non-manual work might indicate a changing relationship between class hierarchies. On both levels the 'teacher' is in a potentially vulnerable position; as a representative of the adult generation relating to the young at a time when young/old relationships are changing and as a representative of non-manual activity particularly exposed to the types of changes in income and status alluded to above.

A third set of changes is within the educational system itself. Raising the statutory leaving age first to 15 and then to 16 has meant the prolongation of the educational experiences of all pupils. Parallel with this, profound changes are taking place in educational objectives, methods and structure. There can be little doubt that the range of objectives of schools has been broadened to include a variety of social and psychological objectives that were either non-existent or ill-defined a generation ago. Similarly the introduction of progressive methods into primary and secondary schools (un-streamed classes, team teaching, subject integration, etc.) has advanced considerably. The reorganisation of a secondary school system on comprehensive lines is a further illustration. It would be surprising if changes as fundamental as this did not affect the characteristics of pupil and teacher relationships throughout the system.

But even here special attention might have to be paid to the inner city school, not because the consequences of these changes are peculiar to it, but simply because they are either more visible or less tolerated in these areas. Forms of behaviour (or types of performance) hidden in the past or tolerated in smaller communities might have higher visibility or low tolerance in the current urban situation.

Let me give an illustration: authorities like the ILEA are currently administering a parallel system of secondary schools, a proportion (it differs from authority to authority but in most LEAs still as many as one pupil in ten is entering a selective school) going to grammar schools and an increasing proportion of the remainder attending comprehensive schools. If we take a situation in which the brightest 12 per cent of pupils enter grammar schools, what is the entry to comprehensive or non-selective schools like? In London a secondary school to which 240 pupils entered each year would have around 40 pupils with a verbal reasoning score of below 80 and another 50 between 81 and 89. Roughly translated into likely performance on a reading or arithmetic test an 8-form entry school would have well over one class of 11-year-olds performing perhaps three years below their chronological age and nearly two other classes perhaps a year and a half below their age. Nearly 40 per cent of the intake would require considerable remedial support and included in that would be 17 per cent performing at a level frequently associated with ascertainment as ESN.

Why labour these points? I do so because I want to suggest behaviour (in this case educational performance) that was invisible or tolerated in some instances may well be becoming intolerable or highly visible in urban centres because of social and educational changes. Poor performance of a 14-year-old in a higher elementary school a generation ago might have remained hidden or taken for granted. Keep him on at school until he is 16, accelerates his physical and certain aspects of social and psychological development by a year and perhaps the situation is different. A 2- or 3-form entry higher elementary school might be able to cope equally well with 10 or 15 very backward pupils per year: I wonder whether an 8- or 12-form entry school could cope equally well with its 40 or 60 such pupils. Evidence put forward by Henry Hodge (see page 81) suggests they cope less well. Further, we ought to discuss the question whether or not an inner city school is able to cope with such numbers as its counterpart in smaller towns. For the typical inner city school, with reorganisation, is likely to be large.

I think two types of changes within the city are relevant to our discussions: first, changes in the population base; and second, changes in the physical base. Changes in the birthrate and migration patterns over the past decade have had a profound effect on the number of people living in certain inner city areas. Again to cite the ILEA: 4,536,000 people lived in the old LCC area in 1901; in 1961 this had fallen to 3,200,000 and by 1971 to 2,775,000. Put in most recent educational terms, in 1960 56,642 births took place in the equivalent of the ILEA, five years later 38,143 pupils entered schools and at the time of transfer to secondary school the size of the 11-plus age group had fallen to 32,366. This is the result of differential migration patterns, and in the future school entry numbers will be affected by recent falls in the birthrate. In 1965/66 nearly 60,000 births took place in inner London, in 1970/71 this had fallen to just over 42,000. The joint effects of migration and fertility will mean that between 1974 and 1981 the projected size of the primary school roll is likely to fall from nearly 200,000 to around 123,000. Peter Newsam considers some of the educational implications of such a change (see page 74).

Concurrent with such changes two other points have been made: one related to ethnic composition of inner city schools, the other to their socio-economic composition. The first point is relatively easy to document. Probably between one-fifth and one-quarter of all pupils in the ILEA have parents born outside the UK and Eire. Although the fact of central areas containing many immigrants is not new, the scale and type of this immigration in the late 1950s and early 1960s is new. The majority of these immigrants come from the New Commonwealth (Asia, Africa, West Indies) and in so far as the fact of racially and ethnically mixed schools raises different educational issues (and these outlast the newness of the migrant) then there has been a significant and sudden change in the educational needs in areas like inner London. In passing it should be pointed out that the decline in performance in ILEA schools is not the result of immigrants: the mean reading score of pupils born in the UK was under 96 and therefore below national norms. More difficult to assess is the changing socio-economic situation of the inner city areas: considerable discussion has taken place on the extent to which inner city areas have become either single-class communities (containing only rich or poor) or have lost the middle part of the social spectrum and become cities of rich and poor. Recent research on the 1966 and 1971 censuses suggests that as far as inner London is concerned, its population has not become less educated or lower class. Nor is it becoming a city of the rich and the very poor. In fact, as Hamnett has noted, there has been 'an overall upward shift in the socio-economic composition of inner London'. Further, this is true not merely on an authority level but also on the level of a ward analysis. Hamnett's concluding sentence is worth quoting: 'the problems manifested in the inner city represent a larger social problem not an urban problem, and purely urban solutions are likely to remain inadequate'.

A final word is necessary on obsolescence of the stock of property (and in this context it is worth mentioning what implications a falling roll of the school population have for replacing obsolete buildings). In 1970 the GLC completed a survey of the condition of London's housing. Around 7 per cent of the houses had been built before 1875 and were therefore 100 or more years old. Around one-third had been built between 1875 and 1919 and so if 60 years is taken as the life of a property these are likely to be obsolete by the end of the decade. In the inner parts the figures were even higher: 14 per cent of the housing stock was built before 1875 and 49 per cent between 1876 and 1919. Therefore nearly two-thirds of these properties on the age criteria of 60 years will be obsolete by 1980. Clearly the age criterion is too crude. Nevertheless, the survey concludes that of the stock of nearly 1 million dwellings in the inner city boroughs 37 per cent were of fair condition or poor and unfit. It was this figure of 37 per cent that they considered could have a useful life of less than 25 years at the time of writing. The problems of replacement of the physical stock of houses together with the replacement of the stock of schools, hospitals, roads, etc. are obviously of relevance to our discussions.

Peter Newsam questions the validity of the previous contributor's assumption that standards of educational attainment are falling, although new arrivals in inner city schools – many of them immigrants – inevitably have problems of adjustment. This questioning of the views of other contributors continues when Newsam takes issue with one aspect of David Eversley's contribution in the first chapter of the book. Eversley argued that a falling population in the inner city has not meant more room for those who remain; but falling school rolls have meant an increase in the amount of space in the schools for those children who remain and, claims Newsam, this is leading to a noticeable falling in tension within those schools. Yet in one respect the following contribution agrees with the general trend of David Eversley's analysis. A fall in school population means higher unit costs. This has been accompanied by a growth in parental power. Falling rolls mean greater choice between schools, and increasingly in some areas parents will be able to close schools by choosing to send their children elsewhere.

2 A counter view – 1 *Peter Newsam*

It is hard enough to understand what is happening in one school; to generalise about many hundreds of urban schools is that much more hazardous. Part of the trouble lies in the information we collect. So far as the quality of education is concerned, this is of two kinds. The first consists of the information derived from such general sources as standardised tests of reading and other skills or from records of examination passes. Where these tests are repeated at the same points in pupils' school careers the results can be used to compare the performance of successive year groups. In the ILEA this monitoring is carried out when children are in the last year of junior school. The second type of information is derived from the performance of individual children over time. These longitudinal studies remain rare but, without them, the effect of teaching in particular ways or types of school cannot be accurately assessed. This means that in our present stage of knowledge even obvious-sounding questions like 'are standards rising or falling?' or 'is this kind of school better than that?' cannot be answered without hedging the answer round with a host of qualifications. Any such qualifications are ignored in public discussion. This in itself makes those who are at the receiving end of most of the misunderstandings, principally teachers and administrators, wary about the whole process.

It is worth exploring a little further how the simple measures which are sometimes all we have can obscure the complex reality they seek to interpret. One actual example will be sufficient. A group of twenty-three children were tested for reading attainment in their third year in the junior school. During the year, three things happened: three of the best readers moved away; the twenty remaining children made some useful progress in their reading; three new children with virtually no English entered the class, and these in turn began to make progress. From the point of view of the teacher, the year's work reflected a high degree of professional skill: everyone's standard had improved. But the mean reading age of the fourth-year children was rather lower than a straightforward comparison with the third-year results suggested would be possible. In that sense, standards were down. This objection would be overcome in studies like the ILEA literacy survey where comparisons are made between the same pupils at different ages and not just between schools, age groups or classes regarded as comparable from year to year. But in the actual situation described it is impossible to answer, in a simple yes or no form, the question 'have standards in this class risen or fallen?'. Whose standards? More important than the answer is what someone might try to do with it. In this instance, for example, it would be wrong for someone in a position of authority to conclude, from a look at the results from the two years, that there is something wrong with the teacher's methods or that greater concentration on reading is needed. This may or may not be true but it cannot be derived from the evidence provided by the tests.

In qualitative terms, there is not much in the way of general statements based on evidence that can be said about urban schools. This is not intended to sound defeatist. It is anyway easy to put too much weight on the usefulness, other than to publicists, of general statements about standards.

Although the question 'what is happening in our schools?' cannot in qualitative terms be directly answered, some useful indicators can be designed. For example, from the various surveys the ILEA has conducted two findings show how what happens in school is being affected by the nature of population movement.

On a sample of some 30,000 pupils, aged 8 in 1968 and 11 in 1971, it was found that despite a considerable movement of population, the social class distributions for all pupils in 1968 and 1971 were similar; if anything the distribution in 1971 was less skewed towards the bottom than in 1968, although the nature of the data means that this finding must be received with caution. Here is at least some counter to the argument heard from time to time that the 'better' people are moving from the inner city and are being replaced by those lower down in the Registrar-General's categories.

Secondly, the mean SRB (reading) score in 1971 of pupils (26,205) who had also been in the 1968 survey was 94·9. The mean score in 1971 of the newcomers since 1968 (5,555) was 90·5. This finding, unlike the previous one, confirms the common assumption. It is after all not surprising that people coming into a system, many from overseas, do less well in it than those who have been here longer. The results went on to show that the mean score of all the pupils in 1968 was 94·6. In 1971, with the numbers leaving balanced by the newcomers, the mean score for all pupils was 94·2. This could be regarded as a fall in standards as the pupils went through the schools or, as London teachers would understandably see it, as a very creditable effort to integrate newcomers while maintaining standards overall. The 1973 stage of this survey, when the children were in the third forms of secondary schools, shows an improvement, in a mean score of 98·0.

Information of this kind helps to interpet what is happening. The paragraphs that follow look first, essentially through London eyes, at other factors affecting schools and then go on to look directly at what is happening within them.

The most important feature of the inner city is the fall in population that is now beginning to be experienced. The ILEA September roll projections illustrate the point:

ILEA (September rolls)	1974	1978	1980	1984
		(thousands)		
Pupils in: primary schools	201	159	140	126
secondary schools	179	173	161	128

Is the fall in numbers to be seen as helpful or otherwise? The point has rightly been made by David Eversley that planners have tended to assume, wrongly he argued in the case of London, that moving people out means more space and other good things for those who are left. Educational planners have often made the opposite assumption and may be equally wrong. Educational planners find increasing numbers, to which they have grown accustomed over the years, both convenient and comforting. They like to build and develop their services. Yet falling numbers may bring educational benefits if properly used.

The outstanding advantage of falling numbers is that they can be used to increase the amount of space available to each teacher and child. The degree to which urban schools are still overcrowded is not widely understood. For example, a recently built London school for 1,700 pupils is on a site of $4\frac{1}{2}$ acres, much of which is taken up by the building itself. This compares with an area of $9\frac{1}{4}$ acres laid down in the building regulations. The degree to which overcrowding contributes to stress is difficult to measure but easy enough to observe. Conversely, where there is enough room for people to move freely, intractable educational problems appear easier to resolve. This can happen quite suddenly; numbers are somewhat reduced, there is somewhat more room and the change becomes apparent. As a community, the school may begin to live and work in a more relaxed and effective way.

A fall in numbers can have important side-effects. Historically there have always been more primary children than secondary ones, sometimes overwhelmingly so: we have grown used to this. As the London figures show, by 1980 this will have changed. Increasingly this will affect teachers: at the moment, numbers of primary and secondary teachers are nearly in balance; but if pupil/teacher ratios in 1980 are, as they are at present, about 1:20 for primary schools and 1:15 for secondary schools, approximately preserving the present differentials, the balance of inner London's teaching force will have changed markedly. Instead of being approximately in balance, there will be 10,600 secondary teachers to 7,200 primary ones. There is, of course, far more to a change of this kind than the number of different kinds of teachers employed. For example, reduced numbers of primary teachers could reduce their influence on an area's educational thinking. Conversely, sufficient primary teachers may move into secondary schools to make their influence more directly felt there than it now is. Either way, this must affect what happens within schools.

One of the most sensible developments authorised by the DES in recent years has been the idea of 'off-programme' building; new school building financed by the sale of old premises. Falling numbers mean that children remaining now have a chance of schools with better physical standards. Already two major developments are planned in London, and there is a chance here for inner city areas to break out of the present deadlock whereby new school building goes to the places where population is rising, and children remaining in areas of static or declining population have to stand by and watch their position relative to others worsening year by year.

Against the one overriding benefit of more and perhaps better space for those who remain there are at least four problems that falling numbers bring. The first is financial. As numbers fall, unit costs tend to rise. London's experience of a fall of 12,000 in the primary school population is that the pro rata saving of £2·75 million that might have been expected in a full year will become an actual saving of £1·6 million in a full year. Schools with somewhat reduced rolls still have to be heated, the rates have to be paid, the roofs mended. In this situation, an education service cannot act abruptly. It cannot suddenly close down plant, as it were, in these participating days even if on educational or financial grounds it was thought desirable to do so. The second problem brought by falling numbers is its effect on the whole planning process; on the possibility of planning itself. The whole tradition in educational planning is based on rising numbers. Schools are built; they become full, and other schools have to be added. Always there is a programme, a looking ahead and a race not to be left too far behind. But the process cannot be reversed when numbers fall. Falling numbers mean a situation that is in principle unstable and to a large extent unpredictable. If it is known now that in five years numbers in an area will have fallen so far that one or more schools in bad premises could close, it ought to be possible, the planners thinks, to say so and plan accordingly. But life is not so simple. To discuss officially and in advance the closure of a school is like talking about devaluation. Either the discussion brings it about too soon, because there is a run on the currency or away from the school, or promises have to be made that it will never happen at all. So the drift continues until there is room to spare in several schools in the area and a growing uncertainty about what is to happen next.

This uncertainty seems essentially an urban phenomenon. Cities will never be the same since events in Paris in 1968. The third problem some would say is the effect of parents and of parental influence in an open market. Students of law look to the Education Acts to find out how schools are closed. In the new situation parents will be able to close schools as easily as education authorities can. If a school, however irrationally, becomes unpopular when there are empty school places near by, it can effectively be shut by an absence of entrants. This can happen quite suddenly and serves to emphasise the irrelevance of most of the talk of legislation or vouchers to give effect to parents' choice of school. When schools are full, legislation is ineffective; one person's preference can be met only at the expense of another's. When schools are empty, legislation is redundant; no one can be prevented from sending a child to a school where there is room.

In the inner city, falling numbers reduce stress and provide new opportunities by improving spatial standards; but these other uncertainties are already arising and their force and effect make for structural instability.

What is happening within the schools themselves? One thing is evident: there is no problem that is not somewhere being successfully tackled. The work of educating in the inner city can be done by ordinary, skilful human beings. The implications of this are important. There is a fashionable disillusion with education which argues that factors outside school are of such importance that what happens within schools can be of little effect. The attitude is catching. It is not unknown to hear people go on to suggest that 'you can't expect much of children with that kind of background'. The refutation lies in the excellence of the work done in some of the schools with, so far as measurement can take us, some of the greatest problems. It is crucial that this should be recognised. It is idle to look for elaborate reasons unrelated to school for the inability, to take one example, of 11-year-old children, suffering from no physical or mental defect, to learn to read when very similar children learn to do so perfectly well in the school down the road. Herein lies the problem. There are wide variations in the quality of inner city education which any averaging process tends to obscure. These variations appear to have little to do with the size of a school or any of its physical characteristics. It is simply that in some schools the ordinary processes of learning and teaching have all but broken down. The picture is familiar and well publicised. Children move in and out, so do the teachers. There is no stability anywhere and the school tends to start each day without any sense of continuity either with its own past or with the whole tradition of teaching that has developed in this country over the past hundred years. In other words, just as there is no problem, however difficult, that is not somewhere being solved so there is no procedure, no obvious element of what constitutes a school, that cannot somewhere be found to be missing. But the essential point is that there are people now in schools showing how the job can be done. Their skills need to be recognised and transmitted to others.

There are some hopeful signs. One development is the growing recognition that a school, primary or secondary, can be seen as a group of teachers with varied skills just as much as a vehicle for transmitting a curriculum. The implications of this are profound for the way improvement is brought about. Increasingly such groups of teachers wish to improve their professional skills in each other's company. The school itself becomes a self-educating community with influences from the outside brought in where necessary.

This is the opposite of the traditional in-service notion which regards training as something that happens to an individual when removed from his working environment. The effect of this thinking on the – in some way opposed – notion of hierarchy will be evident. Management principles, the salary structure, the expectations of parents and the outside world all see the school as in some way hierarchical. Not all schools now feel like this from the inside.

If the skills of a group of teachers are the essence of a school the curriculum loses at least something of its primacy. So too, in the face of falling rolls, does the idea of the entirely self-contained school. Co-operative arrangements between schools are developing fast. These range from consortia of up to ten schools, as in Birmingham, to the joint sixth form arrangements now being initiated in London. Ideas developed from the geographical necessities of Oxfordshire are now very relevant to the inner city. Within schools themselves there are a number of contrary notions at work. First, there is the reluctance to do overmuch measuring of pupils' standards except in their own terms. Thinking in Mode 3 as it were. Meanwhile, from the outside, the desire to hold teachers accountable grows. This is part, perhaps, of the disillusion with education already referred to.

Some people concerned with education never have believed it could do much except for their own children in their own schools. Others thought it could and now are less certain. Both groups wonder whether the educational system is giving good value for money and intend to try to find out. Unfortunately, the more resolutely one presses people to be accountable the more they tend to try to define precisely what it is they are accountable for. The danger is that they will then concentrate too narrowly on achieving these definable measurable objectives to the neglect of others. Hence renewed moves towards defining exactly what the teacher's day should be. A related issue is the way the desire to hold schools accountable, to ensure that they run in a way closely related to clearly defined purposes, is opposed to moves to devolve more and more responsibility for allocating resources in the way best suited to the school to the school itself.

Again there is the tug between what is done within school and what is done outside. There is a general desire to bring more children, however difficult their problems, within the ordinary school. At the same time, as pressures on schools have increased, there is the contrary desire to be rid of those who cause trouble, not just for the problems they themselves represent but also for the effect they have on other children's learning. These two contrary forces are being interestingly combined, in London and elsewhere, in a number of off-site arrangements. For example, at one school a volunteer worker has taken a house near the school and gives accommodation to a teacher who then takes in small groups of eight to fifteen children recommended by the school for full or half-day sessions for varying lengths of time depending on the children's needs. Elsewhere a teacher within a council estate works with children who are reluctant to go to the main school and eventually brings them back into the main school with her. It is the quality of the relationships established within these proliferating arrangements that is their outstanding feature. Though their aims may differ, in this respect they share something of what the free schools represent.

Extended day arrangements are also developing. On the one hand there is the move to define more closely the nature of the teacher's day, its length and the conditions of service under which it is to be worked. On the other, there are a whole range of activities extending in many schools beyond the end of afternoon school. This is not just a matter of games and clubs; the actual development of learning can be impressive.

To sum up: whatever else urban education in England may be it is not static and it is not dull. It cannot be static because the fall in numbers, which in some ways is coming to the rescue, imposes structural uncertainties on the situation and these affect teachers, pupils and administration alike. It cannot be dull because within schools and within the administrative system there are powerful opposing forces at work. These generate tension. Wherever synthesis may lie it is not in the immediate future.

The quality of education in our cities is patchy. Indisputably there are areas of outstanding and largely unrecognised success. So the job of educating inner city children can be done. Where there is failure the reasons are complex and mostly to be found within the school itself. Neither success nor failure can be deduced from the size or type of the school concerned. The quality of something cannot be deduced from its form in education or elsewhere.

In the discussion following Alan Little's paper, Eric Midwinter was quick to point out what he regarded as the fruitlessness of being preoccupied with reading ages in the short term.

3 A counter view – 2 *Eric Midwinter*

Alan Little's persistent assumption that London is somehow part of England confuses me. In the past few years reading ages in Liverpool have risen marginally overall. Reading ages move slightly up and slightly down. After some years of being not too hot, there has recently – according to some evidence – been a marginal rise in Merseyside reading ages. It is marginal; it does not matter an awful lot; but it is certainly not declining. It is not the kind of disaster that he speaks of in terms of the ILEA. Furthermore, I think it is arguable that, certainly over the past 100 years, to take the longer perspective, reading has improved and so has literacy. Given the ambiguities and variables of reading tests in the short term, it would appear to me necessary (at least when one's referential frame is 'the urban crisis') not to become introverted in one's thinking about education and preoccupied with what – over millions of children and generations of time – are tiny shifts in one skill, however important.

Peter Newsam turns our discussion to a point upon which much public discussion is concentrated. In some schools pupils' non-attendance is a very real problem. In other schools it is the attendance of some children that can cause trouble.

4 Indiscipline *Peter Newsam*

The problems that I see are very much those that Alan Little talked about after presenting his paper; the children who do not turn up, the children with major behaviour problems. On the first point he mentioned the 90 per cent attendance in the primary schools. But in the secondary schools, certainly as far as London is concerned, the situation is patchy. Any average that is produced obscures the fact that in a number of schools the situation is serious. It is sometimes assumed that poor attendance means that the school as an organisation is not one that is properly adapted to the pupils' needs. The reality is more complex. The incidence of parents withholding children from school or simply condoning their absence is about twice as frequent as truancy itself.

The other problem, of course, is those who embarrassingly do turn up at school and create trouble. From the outside it is sometimes supposed that the trouble arises because the people inside, the teachers, are at fault, but when you see the kinds of children who are causing the problem you realise that this is by no means the case. In some urban schools teachers are up against problems which are quite intractable.

How big is the problem? Sometimes the problem is put forward as if it were overwhelming and completely incapable of solution. The numbers do not suggest this but they are not easy to interpret. Of one or two schools that I have looked at carefully I have found 20 exceptionally difficult children out of an entry of 300. I know it is argued sometimes that if you take those 20 out there will be another 20, but there really did appear to be 20 children who between them were managing to disrupt the work of their year group. The effective working of comparatively large numbers of children can easily be destroyed by fairly small numbers of them acting in a manner which most of us would regard as so irrational, so unpredictable and so violent that you require somebody watching them almost all the time. Certain senior members of the staff are brought to a state of total exhaustion by sheer nervous worry about what is going to happen if they aren't in the right place at the right time to prevent crisis. It can be as serious as that.

We have already met the assertion that teachers leave schools because the schools themselves are becoming disorganised and ceasing to function effectively, rather than the other way round. In this contribution Henry Hodge, who was for a time chairman of governors of a school in North London, describes how one of these broken-back schools appears to him.

5 A broken-back school *Henry Hodge*

In 1973 I became chairman of the governors of the local comprehensive school. The headmaster had left the year before and the governors had been unable to recommend a suitable candidate for the job after two sets of interviews the previous summer term. Staff shortages were desperate. Ten teachers too few as well as no headmaster. We were sending home over 120 children every day; the parents were understandably furious, the staff were at the end of their tether and the governors could do nothing to help. In protest some of the parents and a few teachers marched on County Hall. The administration was busily trying to help but this action really stirred them up. They put great efforts into staff recruitment and soon had the school back on full-time working, but packed with temporary staff, by mid-October.

The catchphrase for my role seemed to be responsibility without power. Certainly governors play an important part in selecting staff, which is fine so long as there are applicants for jobs, but otherwise the staff and parents look to them for help which it is often impossible to provide. So there were obviously problems with staff, with parents, and of course with the children at the school. How then did these problems develop?

The crucial resource for any school is the people employed there. We were desperate to find a headmaster to provide some focus for reform. We interviewed six candidates in November and although only two were remotely suitable, one was finally appointed to start in the January term. The deputy head, who had held the school together during the worst of the crisis, resigned to leave for a headmastership the next term. So during the rest of the year we had to replace him, four heads of department, three year masters, a number of deputies and numerous teachers. I spent a great deal of my time rushing from work to interviewing committees. We tried to interview as soon as possible after applications closed in order to capture any teachers who might have applied elsewhere. The effect of this turnover on the staff was appalling. They became particularly angry on a couple of occasions because they claimed we were ignoring internal applications for posts of responsibility. They had served their time in the school working in difficult conditions, so the argument went, and they deserved special consideration for this.

On the parents' side, an action group grew out of the troubles. This action group soon decided the governors were the cause of all the problems. They started a newspaper setting out their criticisms. They passed resolutions demanding greater representation on the governing body and the governing body attempted to respond. But the Labour party controls the education division, and although I tried to get the party to appoint some parents to our school board, they were not prepared to let in non-party members. The result of this decision was that we had a lot of cross meetings with the parents' action group.

The rapid teacher turnover also affected the children and discipline seemed to deteriorate. In any event the school was plagued by gangs. In my year as chairman there was a black gang, a white gang, and a mixed gang, all working different kinds of rackets. We were constantly lobbied by groups of teachers about them, and the disciplinary problems that resulted from their activities. One group of teachers said everything would be solved if the governors were willing to suspend really difficult pupils; others were wholly against suspension and thought the school too disciplinarian in any event. When four real troublemakers were suspended it seemed to make no difference, and they were eventually allowed to return.

The school's problems were recognised locally and parents voted with their feet by not putting their children down for the school for 1974/5. As a result the intake went down very considerably, and for the first time the school was undersubscribed in just the same way that Peter Newsam has described (see page 76). Of the new children something like 60 have a reading age of seven, and are therefore in a remedial class. In addition the headmaster thinks that 30 others really ought to be in a remedial class but the facilities do not exist. In total, about half of the new entrants need remedial care. About 25 per cent of the children receive free school uniforms and a very large proportion are in receipt of free school dinners. The children suffer because there are too many low-ability children in the annual intake. Instead of the staff being happy about the smaller numbers, as it is suggested they ought to be, they are all angry as the reduction will affect their points next year, with commensurate cut in the school's budget.

Despite these difficulties the school is improving, primarily because stability has returned to the staff. We have appointed a number of new young teachers; the headmaster has a senior management team and although their main role seems to be to walk around the school, to drag people out of the lavatories, stop them smoking and make them pick up pieces of paper, none the less the atmosphere is noticeably better than when I first had to deal with the problems of short-time working.

In the final contribution in this section we draw from the recorded interviews made in a college of further education of pupils' impressions of life in an inner city secondary school. While they make no pretence of being drawn from a random sample, they do vividly highlight the failure of some schools to provide the basic organisation necessary for learning.

6 Consumers' reactions

Edited by Patricia Haikin

1. *George*

The form master that we had was a hard teacher. If we ever done anything wrong, he thought it was up to him to sort us out and when I mean sort us out, he really did, you know. So, you know, he'd never take us down to the headmaster and just have a talk in. He'd get a belt out that he used to have and then hit us with that. I suppose it was going back to the old way of school which was a bit bad I think. But then, when we had to walk around the school to have our lessons, it got a bit tempting to bunk off so that was what we did. But those lessons that we did go to I think it was about one in every three, and second year which was pretty bad, because we'd never learn anything, you know. I remember one time that we were supposed to have French lessons and in the one term we had about 10 teachers and really we'd only had two lessons in it. At the end of the second year all we could say in French was from one to ten. About the third year when all we was doing was art and games, you know, and everyone else was bunking off, there didn't seem to be many at school, apart from the Greeks who done anyone up who did stay at school; so it was pretty bad. That's the main reason I left really.

I got done six times on the trot you know; one day after the other, and had nearly every bit of money I had nicked. And I wore a coat to school for the first time and then that got ripped; then I was stabbed in the arm. You know, I'm not just saying this about me, but I'm just giving you the general view. I know a lot of mothers, you know, they pulled their kids away because they were stabbed and all that and then as soon as they got to other schools, they found it to be worse.

So that was the general outlook. So then I left there, mostly through kids beating me up and everything, and the lessons were no good and the teachers were never there, so I just went to work in a shop. So that really everything I tried to learn at school was never any good to me anyway because all I ended up doing was filling shelves.

2. *Tom*

I never used to go that much to school because I didn't used to like it. But when I used to (I was there about three quarters of the time) we used to have English with a Mr Silver and all we used to do was run out, mucking about, running round the corridors and that, flying aeroplanes out the windows on people and things like that and in the fourth year, that was all right. That was like all technical stuff like brickwork, metalwork, technical drawing and that – the only strict teacher in school was the teacher in brickwork. Like, if you used to play about, he'd throw a brick at you or a bit of mortar. Never used to mean to hit you but just right near your head. Not a whole bit, just a bit of it. He was all right, but a bit of a nutter. He used to go a bit mad and was about the only teacher in the school that would make you take notice of him. No one else really, 'cos I was really frightened of him. He was all right when you talked to him and that, but if you used to do something wrong, he used to go mad. Woodwork was all right. We used to make things like bedside cabinets, and things like that.

In science there was a Yugoslavian bloke and he couldn't speak a word of English. We never used to learn anything and his writing was upside down and all his letters were, you know, right really small. Couldn't read a word of what was on the blackboard and if you couldn't understand it, he used to go mad. He used to expect you to do it perfectly and he knew we couldn't understand it but – and the head of science, he knew we couldn't understand him either, but he was on his side you know, and just said we was mucking about all the time. I didn't like the science and I never used to go that much.

English was all right. In the first three years I used to do good essays and things like that. Then in the fourth year I knew I was going to leave at Easter, so I started mucking about and you know, just making aeroplanes out of books and all that.

Maths was no good. We used to have Mr Thompson, some big black bloke and he used to give you the stick for the slightest little thing and all the people were scared of him but they still never used to do no work 'cos he was the head of maths and he used to go round to the other class and make sure they was doing their work. And when he was out we used to put pins on his chair and put books on top of the door so they all come down on his head. One time we done that the headmaster walked in and it hit him on the shoulder but he never said anything. Everyone started laughing. I still don't like maths now really.

Then we went down to Mr Robson. He was second head of science like, and he used to look after his pond in the school and I used to help him clean it out. That was one way of getting out of work and I used to get all the tadpoles and things like that, put them in this aquarium until they grew some little ones and put them back again. And that was all right that was, and then after that I left.

The school wasn't really understaffed. There wasn't one time when we went to school there wasn't a teacher to take us. In the fourth year I knew I was going to leave at Easter so I didn't really worry about going to school. I used to go round this library and I could learn more in there really, just reading books and things like that, football books, you know, things like that. I read books about getting jobs and that, that's what made me leave school. I didn't really hate school, but I like work much better than school.

3. Brian

The school was a secondary modern. Teachers were knifed and it was very rough. It was a school that no one really wanted to go to. We were forced really to go to the school. You didn't have much of a choice: just a choice between two schools. So when we turned up, we was a bit apprehensive about what would happen. Well, we had nothing but films for three quarters of the day because there was so many teachers understaffed. And we was all going in the gym, about 80 people in the gym for PE and weird things like that. After about the first six or seven months it became a bit better. More teachers were coming in. You had more regular teachers for regular lessons. You didn't sort of get one teacher for a lesson, then get a different teacher next week for the same lesson. A lot of the older teachers left, being the school's a bit of a roughhouse. Then they divided the school up into first two years in the front building, and the third, fourth and, if anyone wanted to do a fifth year, in another building. So the first and second year building was the much quieter building.

A lot of the old teachers left, the old battle-axes and we had quite a few young ones, about 22, 23 – must have just come out of college with new ideas. So the second year was quite enjoyable. Discipline wasn't too bad – you had a fair headmaster you saw a lot. He was in assembly every morning and you could see him during the day if you wanted to, so he didn't seem so far off. The third year – well, that was a year to remember. We had quite a few new teachers coming. Most of them were very young students, all trying to show how big they were. Eventually all the really bad ones were taken out of the school and the good ones were left.

We had a Maori teacher who was quite funny, Australian, Nigerian – we had quite a selection of teachers, you know, from all different countries. We had a change of headmaster to a man called Mr Thompson who was Scottish and had some quite weird ways. He was all for new ideas but he was never in the school to carry them out. In the fourth year, which was supposed to be an examination year, the school quietened down quite a bit. All the vandals and bigheads were put in one class. They had a streaming system, which was a G class, A class, B class, C class and a class called the Outer Remove which is a bit of a horrible name to put on a class like that. I was in the A which is supposed to be second from the top, but there wasn't really much difference between the first three classes.

The fourth year was quite a year. They had a couple of real clean-up campaigns, anti-jean weeks, where everyone wearing jeans was sent home to get changed. Everyone wore jeans and got sent home, so they had to drop that idea because it wouldn't work. They tried to enforce a school uniform which we didn't want to wear because we wanted to be our individual ways. You know, there seemed to be no really good reason, they said something about everyone looking the same but no one really wants to look all the same nowadays.

At the end of the fourth year we took exams called College of Preceptors, which are harder than CSEs. We got a fair amount of training for that, but then again the teachers were quite good in some subjects, but others, they lacked a bit of go in them. They were just too willing to give us a book and tell us to get on with it and no real teachers who were willing to do a bit of hard work.

After the end of the fourth year, I decided to stay on for an extra year to try and get some exams. The way I was going in the fourth year I thought it would be quite easy to get a few O levels at least. This seemed to be a good idea at the time, but afterwards I realised it was the biggest waste of time I've ever done. The school went comprehensive. It joined up with a school which is a grammar school. It was a new building built about 1940. The one we was in already was built about 1927 – quite an ancient monument. We had a new extension on the back, which had all new ultra-modern classrooms – not really modernly built, nor very soundproof. They had the metal workshop right next to the technical drawing classes, so it was a bit of a noisy atmosphere. Going to do your examinations that year – it's a nasty year to have to change over; being used to all your same teachers and getting completely different teachers. Well, we came back from the summer holidays a day earlier to get settled in a bit better, you see, give us a bit more of a chance. When we got there it was absolutely silly. No one knew what they were doing. The teachers were in a virtual trance. It wasn't well planned. They started planning it nine months before it was due to happen and they still couldn't get it correctly planned. I thought the idea of the comprehensive system was that the streaming was completely lost but without any of us being told, they kept all the grammar school students in their own classes, right the way through. Well the top class, which is the G class, they just kept intact. They didn't bother trying to blend them. Our class was lumbered with all the stupid blokes, you know, who were really a bit dumb and who just continually mucked about.

Well, it wasn't because the way we mucked about; it was just that the County High boys kept all their same teachers and got some of ours. If their history teacher wasn't so well qualified as our one, they'd get our history teacher. So we was given virtually the dirt of the teachers.

4. *David*

I used to go to a secondary modern school. Actually it's two schools for they're separated in different places. One school is the lower school and the other is the upper school. Separated schools to me is more like having two different schools. But first when I went to school it was ever so odd, because there were ever so many coloured people going to the school at that time. A couple of years later, if you go there the school's nearly all coloured people because it's the way the place is situated in Hackney and lots of coloured people are living there.

The standard of teaching there is very poor because you often had a class and the teacher couldn't understand what you were saying, so they said: 'Oh well, you'll never learn it. So sit down and be quiet', and you're never told anything. You're told to sit there and listen. Okay, but can you learn by listening all the time? – can't ask any questions. Most coloured people's problem's mostly with the language. Not so much speaking but say putting it on paper.

In this English class in the lower school it was very bad, because the teacher said: 'You try it yourself', and you couldn't do it, and you were told: 'Well, try a bit harder.' You were given homework and you couldn't do the homework, he'll say: 'What's this then? That's right. You're supposed to be at home doing your homework.' You say, 'But I can't do it,' and he's not explained to you in any sort of way so you can understand and you're able to do it.

In my first year it was hard for me because when I came over here the teaching standard was different to mine. I started woodwork and

I had been doing it and when the teachers realised I was good they said: 'Ah, we give you woodwork all the time', and that was it. And they give you half a day, one morning full of woodwork and about half an hour's English and PE and that is the lot. I think that's ridiculous. It's things like English or maths you need, which wasn't taught to you, but they were giving you what you already knew so there wasn't much point in teaching you.

Afterwards I realised they didn't care much about what you did and what you didn't do as long as they got their pay. That's all we were hearing. As long as we get our pay, never mind – couldn't care less. 'We'll get our pay in a month, we're not losing anything.' He always said we didn't do as we were told because we wasn't listening, but how do you expect to write and even if you was listening it would just come through one ear and out the other because you didn't know what they were on about. So how can you learn something when you don't know what he's on about? You're supposed to be taught in simple terms so you can understand them.

I moved to the upper school in the fourth year. Making a change was like changing to a different school because you had to get used to the atmosphere – I mean, with kids older than you. Maths and English was pretty bad because some of the teachers didn't turn up. They couldn't care less as usual. But I think it's not really their fault but sometimes it was ours. On mornings coming for registration we hardly ever had a teacher. Our teacher was supposed to be there. She was never there. We was being substituted with a different teacher every morning and we couldn't get used to one teacher before we changed. And this is bad because other classes get on with their form teachers and they're okay. But our form was in a mess. Our class was always in trouble. Someone in our class every day was in trouble. It couldn't be helped. Because I think we had no one to sort of look after us. We needed to be guided the right way instead of into trouble. The first place they came to was our class, because we had no teacher and they couldn't care less.

Most of the bad parts have been said about teachers but that's because I'm a student but most of it was the teachers – I won't say the teachers' fault primarily, but I will say some of it was ours because some of us didn't care because we weren't taught to care in the first year or anything like that. We were just taught to mess around, do this, do that. So when it came to English, we couldn't do it. What we should have done in the first, second and third year we hadn't done and how can we jump those stages and do something harder then? We didn't even do the basic part. It's supposed to be for my sake but it wasn't because I wasn't being taught the things I need to know. They were really for listeners, following. I could never follow and fell asleep. As it gets so boring I don't find it feeling interesting. I couldn't learn a thing in that English lesson because no one was interested in the lesson. I mean, just boring, just sat there – no work. He just continued reading and we all just fell over slowly. So I couldn't be bothered with the lesson. I said: 'That's it. That's my lot.' So I'm afraid I can't really say I've learnt anything in English. When people come over here that's their weakest point – most West Indians – because some of them don't catch on.

We had a subject called physics and we had a weird teacher. Don't know what kind of bloke he was. But he was bad. At first I wasn't keen on learning physics and we had another bloke who was there before. He wasn't much good at teaching because all you did was copy from the blackboard. He just spent all the lesson writing on the blackboard over and over and we had to copy it. And we didn't learn – at least I didn't learn anything. It came to a stage where I couldn't do something and I said, 'Can I ask you for some help?' and he just said to me, 'If you don't get it now, you won't get it by the end of the year.' So he kept going on and going on about this so I said to him, 'Well how do you expect me to learn it if you're not teaching me?' So I said to him well he can get lost because I'm not learning anything from you. I was thrown out of the class. As soon as I arrived in a class for physics the first thing was out of the door for me. All I had to do was open my mouth and I was out. It's not so much the building as the people who are in the school that makes the school, like I mean, like people, like people who go to the school and teachers.

Well actually – I can't say I've got something out of school because I haven't got much. All the things I need I didn't get, like maths and English. I got woodwork but that's about all I got out of it, I didn't get nothing else. It's been a hard time for me.

4

A New Deal for Urban Education

Before the conference began its discussions on possible reforms of urban education, delegates considered the demands that some parents are currently putting forward. Both Alan Little and Virginia Makins maintained that the overriding demand from parents was that children should be able to read and write and that schools should be safe and peaceful places. The argument is then developed in two ways by Harriett Wilson. In the first place she points out that demands of many parents run counter to progressive educational thinking. She then draws the attention of the conference to the new skills needed by teachers since the Plowden revolution in primary school teaching. Eric Midwinter develops this point still further under the heading of 'The new professionals'.

1 What do parents want?

(a) Gaining basic skills *Alan N. Little*

I have not met a single parent any here who does not want his or her child to read or do its sums. I think most people's expectations of their children and the way they judge their schooling are very conventional. Whether you or I like it or not, I put on one side. People's educational judgments are conventional and these are the expectations that I am trying to report. For example, whether a child at the age of nine ought to be able to say 'The cat sat on the . . . [underline the word "mat"]' – I should say that 95 per cent of the Great British public would say 'Yes, I want the child to underline the word "mat" '; 5 per cent of the trendies may not, but the vast majority want 'mat' underlined.

Virginia Makins

Is it that complicated, what parents want to get out of a school? Peter Newsam was saying that the influence of parents was one of the new points in this situation, in London anyway; that they were now beginning to make their demands felt in very simple terms of not closing that school because they liked it, or closing another one, because they would not send their children there. It seemed to me that Alan Little was right in saying that parents want their children to learn reading and the allied skills with which this is correlated. I also think that parents want schools to be safe and peaceful places for their children. A great many of them are not that at the moment.

(b) Parental attitudes *Harriett Wilson*

How do parents see school and its aims? In a study of low-income families with five or more children who live in inner-ring areas of a large Midlands city the majority of mothers had no clear views on the objectives of education and showed little awareness of what goes on in the classroom (Harriett Wilson and G. W. Herbert, *Parents and Children in the Inner City*, Routledge & Kegan Paul, forthcoming). School and its values were accepted uncritically, and mothers tended to back up teachers as persons of authority. Contacts with school were generally limited to one or two parents' meetings a year; very few mothers established more personal contacts by visiting school when they felt particularly worried, or when a teacher asked to see a mother for a special reason. This pattern was found to be typical of families in general who are resident in EPA-type areas. In a random sample of 389 indigenous boys from the catchment areas of the research only 10 per cent of parents were rated by teachers as 'taking the initiative in discussing the child's progress', or as 'supporting the school's efforts in an active way'. The percentage is somewhat higher for infant school children than for juniors. This information must not be seen as a valid measure of parental interest in their children's education. We found in interviews with parents that difficulties in communication and social insecurity play a large part in determining contact between home and school. The passive, accepting attitudes of the majority of parents reflect a history of exclusion from the rewards of education. School failure was an experience shared by most of the parents and was seen as a fact of life. In that way an adaptation to unequal opportunities was made.

In contrast to the majority of mothers, a small group were very critical of school. Their complaints were about unfair treatment of their children, not enough for dinner, other children bullying or bashing their own, coloured kids who smell, teachers picking on the kids, teachers not being strict enough, teachers not using the cane often enough, teachers caning the kids too often for trivial reasons, the kids never bringing homework home, the kids always bringing books home which only get ripped up. There were also specific accounts of teachers not responding sympathetically. These mothers tended to see teachers as no different from other people, and the points made by them reflect an unwillingness to grant teachers the authority of parents while the child is in school. Parental involvement in school affairs by this small group expressed itself vigorously in all directions. It is obvious that, if such involvement is desired, it would need to be channelled into constructive approaches.

(c) Parental involvement *Harriett Wilson*

Parental involvement in children's education may be good in itself, but it is usually seen as desirable because of its association with higher attainments of the children at school. J. W. B. Douglas (*The Home and the School*, MacGibbon & Kee, 1964) found that working-class children tended to work well when their parents took an interest in their school progress and to work badly when their parents were uninterested, but middle-class children were less influenced by their parents' attitudes and tended to work hard even when their parents lacked interest. The Plowden Council, convinced that the association of parental interest and attainments at school is causally connected – at least in the case of working-class parents – recommended a programme of increased parent–teacher communication. The Halsey study (*Educational Priority*, vol. 1, HMSO, 1972) incorporated the Plowden recommendation by making one of its four objectives 'to increase the involvement of parents in their children's education'.

Increased parental involvement as such does not necessarily result in harmonious relations with school staff, or improved functioning of their children. Halsey, well aware of the potential culture clash in the educational priority area, points out that 'ideas, values and relationships within the school may conflict with those of the home, and [that] the world assumed by teachers and school books may be unreal to the children' (ibid., p. 43). When it comes to reinforcing or perpetuating 'values and attitudes which would be widely regarded as undesirable, moral judgments have to be made about the ways of life that the schools should support and those they should try to change' (ibid., p. 118). If this is to be part of a teacher's assignment one may well ask: are teachers in training being prepared for such moral judgments, and if they are, what are the moral judgments to be?

The Plowden Council was deliberately vague. It was assumed that a child progresses naturally through a series of developmental stages into maturation, and this led the Council to observe that a 'culturally deprived' child may 'miss a significant stage in his early social development. Children who have been reared in this way often find difficulty in handling their impulses and needs' (*Children and Their Primary Schools*, vol. I). In other words, the approach to problems of children in EPAs was seen in terms of individual maladjustment in a community which shares the normative traditions of mainstream society. For that reason the Council did not feel it necessary to make explicit the aims of primary education except in very generalised terms: 'to be adaptable and capable of adjusting to their changing environment . . . to be able to live with their fellows . . . and to be able to withstand mass pressure' and so on. As Peters pointed out, the ideology of self-directed growth of the child towards autonomy could be disastrous if it is not accompanied by a well-defined set of values: 'What is one to make of this emphasis on being oneself? . . . it is a vacuous recommendation which is consistent with any form of development; for presumably the Marquis de Sade was being himself as much as St Francis. They just had different selves to develop' (*Perspectives on Plowden*, Routledge & Kegan Paul, 1969).

The effect which the Plowden ideas have had on the younger generation of teachers is described in a study of 1,500 primary teachers (P. Ashton, P. Kneen, F. Davies and B. Holley, *The Aims of Primary Education*, Macmillan, 1975). In contrast to their older colleagues the younger teachers tended to want children to develop their own attitudes towards society and their chosen way of life, organise their own time and set their own goals. While older teachers tended to stress moral and spiritual development, plus training in traditional skills, the younger teachers thought that emotional and personal development were the most important aspects of the aims of education. The Plowden way of thinking thus appears to have had an impact on the way younger teachers define their roles. Pre-Plowden teachers tend to see themselves as agents of transmission of traditional values, including well-defined skills; to read fluently, accurately and with understanding, to write clear and meaningful grammatical and correctly spelt English, to do arithmetical computations, etc. Their moral values included obedience, industriousness, persistence and conscientiousness. The younger teachers did not consider these to be the major aims of primary education. Instead, they wanted to see the children happy, well balanced, enthusiastic and eager. The authors remark that this study was no more than an initial exploration of a relatively uncharted area which, they hope, will be widely debated, as the findings led them to conclude that there had not been an evolution of thought in education but 'a reaction of one tradition against another'.

In the meantime, the children in EPA schools and elsewhere who come from poor homes with low educational aspirations are being taught by these primary teachers. Whether the typical pre-Plowden teacher or the typical post-Plowden teacher is better able to make the moral judgments which Halsey demands is answered by Ashton and her colleagues, but we are left guessing which of the two is likely to be more sympathetic towards the deprived child.

(d) The new professionals *Eric Midwinter*

I want to develop the point about the new professional, the new teacher which Harriett Wilson has just raised. It seems to me that the role of the teacher has to be overturned, or is in the process of being overturned. I will summarise my views along the following lines.

The teacher is becoming and will have to become a social explorer and social critic rather than a social defender. The teacher has normally been forced by society to take up a kind of Casabianca-like stand, like the boy on the burning deck 'whence all but he had fled', defending mores which society itself has abandoned. Because of the state of our knowledge about the influence of the environment, particularly the home and the family, on educational attainment in its purest sense as well as other aspects, the teacher will need to become an adult educator in the very broadest sense as well as a child educator. This is a really difficult role for many teachers to take as they are just not trained to do it.

When we first started this kind of work six or seven years ago there was a tendency for teachers to say, 'We don't want those dirty, bloody, smelly mothers in here with us. Our job is to get the children away from the mothers and get some sums into them.' More and more teachers are now saying, 'Yes, we understand the principle. We accept the argument of increased parental involvement without reservation. How do we do it? No one ever told us how to do it.'

It is possible to get through a three-year course in a college of education without hearing the word 'parent' mentioned in anger. I am also told that it is now possible to do a four-year course for a B.Ed. without hearing the word 'child' mentioned in anger. I think that is a rumour; it is like the housing shortage – it is a rumour spread about by those who have nowhere to live. This points very compellingly in the direction of training.

As the fences and gates of schools tumble, and the school ventures into its host community, entering into dialogue with its catchment community, the teacher has got to become something more of a public craftsman than a private tutor. For the teacher this is a tremendous change in the style of what he is doing. I think this change in style, of being the conductor of the educational orchestra, has not been rated highly enough. This was brought home to me when I was talking about an exhibition we held at the big store, T. J. Hughes. We had about 10,000 visitors to that exhibition in about twelve days. As well as exhibiting school work and having an education shop, we staged a live demonstration. Classes of children were taught in the store so that parents and others could observe the process. The teachers also talked to the people and explained what they were doing.

I have often told the tale of the probationer teacher who brought a class of 40 infants in and arranged a PE lesson in front of a crowd of 300 shoppers. When I recall this incident to students and teachers there is always a great sigh of wonderment and 'Wasn't she brave?' and 'That girl had guts as well as gifts.' I included this incident in a recent talk which was not just to teachers and students; other people had managed to infiltrate – business people, local government officers of one kind and another. They were quite unmoved by this tale of courage and devotion beyond the call of duty. One of the audience said to me: 'What are you making such a fuss about it for? The shop girls at T. J. Hughes do their job all day long in front of hundreds of shoppers. What is so special about you teachers that you have constantly got to be working behind closed doors?' I thought that that was a very salutary question to raise, for I could not think of an answer. I raise it again. I think that we have talked a lot about the teacher as a social explorer in terms of curriculum. We have talked a great deal about the necessity for the teacher to relate with the parent. But this question is also very important.

The conference then turned its attention to the relationship between the educational system and the labour market. Nicholas Gillett begins the discussion by reminding us of the huge variety of jobs which make up the inner city labour market. In the following contribution he argues that community schools in the inner city are much better placed than the more conventional school in responding to the demands of their

*local labour market. It is important for all inner city schools to have
well-trained and well-informed careers teachers. The number of jobs is
not static. Good knowledge and contact with the local labour market
can result in a greater proportion of students being placed in
employment.*

2 Schools and the labour market

(a) Making people employable *Nicholas Gillett*

What constitutes the inner city's job market? The area is close to the
infinite variety of jobs requiring skill or no skill at all which may be
expected in a commercial centre. Birmingham may pride itself on
being the city of a thousand trades but any great city is a city of a
thousand different kinds of job. Government publications have
listed such unlikely occupations as makers of pips for raspberry
jam. For the more daring there are skyscraper windows to clean.
Those with confidence can always invent new jobs, but for most the
trouble lies deep. The young man who has lost his first job, because
he has continued to play truant or arrive late, as he may have done
at school, stands on the street corner and for him the thousand
trades may mean a thousand closed doors. He is not like the illiterate
eleven-year-old in a Birmingham inner city school who was allowed
to set up a lathe in the front room of his home and later became
such a skilled apprentice that he was chosen to demonstrate to the
Duke of Edinburgh. Nor is he in the position of a porter at the Gare
du Nord where only relatives are employed as all tips are shared.
He does not know the right people and frequently rejects the help
of the Youth Employment Officer. Where families break up, the old
boy network of the poor breaks up and no one knows whether a
particular applicant can be left working in a customer's private
house or whether he can be trusted with money and so he may go
jobless, though his help is badly needed, because he has no one to
vouch for him.

The job market within half an hour's travel from the inner city
areas of Manchester, Birmingham, etc. defies statistical description
even if it is only unskilled jobs which are in question. Looked at
in one way there is something infinitely depressing or even sordid
about them, though it would be difficult to describe the jewellery and
gun quarters of Birmingham this way. Looked at through the eyes
of Dickens they would seem very different; he would have cast a
glow of whimsicality about every workshop new or old, like the old
family business on a street corner in Bristol which exchanged hands

in a canoe on the Cherwell at Oxford. No doubt the pleasure in the work arises partly from meeting people more than once so as to establish a relationship with them and this is more difficult in some city centre jobs, but with shops, catering, the entertainment industry and transport as well as factories to choose from, there is likely to be the right niche for the ordinary leaver if only it could be found.

Those who have most difficulty in the job market are frequently those who have had most difficulty at school and at home. Dealing with truancy and lateness whether by teachers or parents is vocational education *par excellence*, though it may not be fashionable to say so. An ability to follow written and oral instructions, an adaptability to new circumstances, team loyalty and honesty with money are examples of traditional school virtues which teachers recognise more often as linked to school rather than of importance to the young employee.

Having claimed in this brief introduction that it is necessary to beware of neat concepts of inner city areas and of job markets to which they have access, it is permissible to clarify the assumption that schools near city centres producing large numbers of unskilled and semi-skilled workers in comparison with others do exist and need to establish a policy relevant to their individual circumstances. Writers such as Blaugh and Vaizey provide a chill reminder that a 'good' education leading to life on the street corner is to be deplored. If the wage structure is subject to monopoly influences so that many workers are no longer worth their hire, a challenge is presented to schools and industrial training systems to raise the standard of economic efficiency to match the wage structure.

Coombs puts a similar point in a different way:

A central assumption underlies the conviction – now widely shared by educators and economists – that education is a good investment in national development. The assumption is that the educational system will produce the kinds and amounts of human resources required for the economy's growth, and that the economy will in fact make good use of these resources. But suppose the opposite happens? Suppose the educational system turns out the wrong mix of manpower? Or suppose it turns out the right mix but the economy does not use it well? What then? Doubts then arise about education's productivity and the efficacy of the investment made in it. (P. H. Coombs, *The World Educational Crisis: a Systems Analysis*, Oxford University Press, 1968.)

It is easier to ask questions than to answer them, and there is little help from the manpower planners for the individual school. Educational planning is a characteristically un-British activity since it assumes that educational power lies with Ministers of Education rather than with headmasters. However, something can be done to bridge the gap. In 1934 Tawney gave 166,000 as the number of unemployed juveniles between the ages of fourteen and sixteen and nevertheless denounced those who employed school leavers for a few years at a time as exploiting waves of cheap labour. This figure contrasts with the unduly optimistic 1,300 as the number of fifteen-year-olds leaving without a job in 1971. The optimism arises from not taking into account the report suggesting that half the young unemployed black people were not registered at careers offices or employment exchanges, apparently because they did not see this as a way to a job (Community Relations Commission, *Unemployment and Homelessness*, HMSO, 1974).

In any case prospects for 1976 are bad and it is worth studying the Council of Europe report to form some idea of possible misfits between education and the job market (*Unemployment Among Young People*, HMSO, 1972). It indicates that in several countries despite more people going on to higher education a greater percentage of the rest is unemployed. The debate whether advancing technology demands more or less skill from the labour force continues, but many employers prefer their employees to have unnecessary qualifications, partly as an indication of hard work at school, partly to have a reserve of relatively adaptable labour. The famous large bookshop with a firm rule against the employment of graduates is exceptional.

In the next few years the inner city school will have to take its careers work much more seriously than in the past. It needs to be stated that there is not a fixed number of jobs to be filled but that careful matching of job to applicant or vice versa may create a post additional to any advertised. A harassed shopkeeper had been upset by the flighty behaviour of two or three previous assistants and had decided to manage without one. A teacher suggested he was appointing the wrong kind of person and persuaded him to spend twice as long patiently explaining the work to a very slow learner. She proved to be as punctual and loyal as she was slow in picking up the job.

Normally a proportion of inner city children need this kind of extra help. The area may be going downhill or, on the Islington pattern, going up but in either case social bonds are few. Turbulence, the moving in and out of the area is usually high, one-parent families form a high proportion of the whole. Grandparents and teachers live a long way away so that the social workers are over-burdened. Some of these statements are not based on hard evidence but on guesses drawn from one source or another, which require further investigation; nevertheless on this framework the remainder of this paper depends: firstly work in schools, secondly the less formal education which takes place outside the school curriculum and thirdly the selection and education of teachers.

The formal careers advice provided by Youth Employment Officers and Careers Teachers has been described elsewhere in detail. Two-thirds of secondary schools, according to the DES Report on Careers Education (HMSO, 1972), have careers education on the timetable. It may be guessed that the remaining third serve areas with little choice of job, or inner city areas where ambition is low and leavers assume they will enter unskilled jobs. It might be added that only 11 per cent of careers teachers have attended a course of one term or longer so as to know their job thoroughly. On the whole the Youth Employment Services fit the inner city school least well, since the leavers are unresponsive to suggestions from official sources and frequently hold a job for a relatively short time. Inner city leavers aspire to jobs rather than careers and tend to choose higher wages in the immediate future in preference to apprenticeships which may offer more in the long run.

A school may do a great deal by establishing an ethos and authority structure which make life in a factory or office comprehensible. Some of the relationships need to be underlined or made explicit. Perry draws a fine line by writing 'Any subject matter can be viewed as suitable either for education or training. . . . Limited or general applicability is a mark of distinction between training and education' (L. R. Perry, 'Training and education', *Philosophy and Education Society Proceedings*, 6 January 1972). He suggests educationists might study: (*a*) why transfer of skills from one situation to another often fails; (*b*) why training turns into education in institutions organised for training; (*c*) why education turns into training in institutions organised for education.

He might have added a comment in line with the Schools Council's Working Paper no. 33 that it is difficult for young people to adjust to widely differing atmospheres in the space of one day (*Choosing a Curriculum for the Young School Leaver*, Evans and Methuen, 1971). Does this encourage a desirable flexibility? It would be tactless for an ambitious social studies teacher to discuss with the children the pupil–teacher relationships within the school. On the other hand it is not entirely convincing to set up institutions for industrial training which are as nearly as possible half-way between schools and factories, as in Holland. Here the training is liable to drive out the education.

It would be presumptuous to claim to be able to understand the many factors, some of them subtle, which go to produce the ethos of a school. There have in one century or another been school buildings which might have been mistaken for humble homes, chapels and palatial country houses. Nowadays it requires a skilled eye to pick them out from offices and factories. Inside them the regimes have been equally distinctive but those of the inner city schools which are in old buildings are in a class apart. With their high windows they seem to have been built to allow Bernard Shaw to write the famous lines which begin 'Schools are like prisons only worse'. The teacher–pupil relationships which accompany such schools have been aptly described by Eric Midwinter, writing of areas where teachers motor each morning through enemy-occupied territory to reach 'their' schools. Though he qualifies the implications of this statement elsewhere (*Projections*, Ward Lock, 1972, p. 39) as well as denoting a change in attitudes of some teachers (see page 94), it is nevertheless apparent that the valiant two-year-trained teachers speaking with the local accent had an advantage over many contemporary young teachers.

The ethos of the school should beget confidence. If the school aims to allow everyone to be good at something it will confer a lasting benefit on its pupils. This may be done, for example, by introducing the highly successful exhibitions of things made and done at home. Unsuspected talent even among the less gifted is always discovered, a new basis is found for learning by children who have lost interest in formal education and parents are attracted into the school as by nothing else. Pupils learn what people they should go to for help and parents see what scope needs to be provided at home so that the general handiness appreciated by employers is acquired.

Another way of according recognition to all is the 'Record of Personal Achievement'. This is filled in by the young person whenever he does something in school or out which he is pleased to tell his teachers and prospective employers. It was planned originally in co-operation with Swindon employers and has been running so successfully that already eighty schools outside Swindon have adopted the scheme.

Many schools simulate interviews with employers, but this often provides an example of turning into training what might be education. In geography, teachers are apt to forget the limits of the geographical experience of the average class member and talk about snow-capped mountain ranges as though they had any under-standing beyond what television can bring. Similarly the range of acquaintances who have had an influence on the children during the course of their growing up may be much more limited than teachers assume. Many children may have heard a grandparent tell a story about their childhood, some have not even had this experience. Few have talked with anyone who has lived overseas so as to be able to compare, however roughly, two ways of living. They may even have acquired the prejudice that 'different' in this context means worse rather than interesting. Similarly, few have had the chance to hear a plumber, electrician or other skilled worker talk about the jobs he has done and follow up with questions. The teacher can bring such people into the classroom or encourage spare-time contacts so as to improve the social network, help people out of their cells of privacy or their age-group gangs. It is a clear example of improving general education and preparing people for the job market simultaneously. The tongue-tied sales girl and the plumber's mate who cannot understand what the house-owner means are difficult to employ. There is also a very rich significance in Martin Buber's 'I and Thou' at the simpler school-leaver level. The awareness of other people of the Cockney humorist makes him what he is.

In practical classroom terms more school work can be based on the weekend and holiday jobs which are undertaken. In the USA elaborate work books to be filled in by pupils are used. Homework can take the form of finding out from adults about their jobs with a view to writing or reporting at school. Local studies might be much more closely linked to local jobs. Careers literature looks so glossy it unfortunately outshines the more important school-made brochures about what goes on in local firms. It can be argued that every school subject can be found somewhere in a factory, and yet the bridge is not made because even teachers fail to take the point.

Beyond this schools can give a place of honour to practical work and skill by the exhibitions held. Practical homework can be en-couraged in such a way that the efforts of the teachers flow over into the homes by capturing the support of parents. More teaching can best be done by teaching through parents instead of against them and a reformed PTA has an important role to play.

In the course of the local studies, visits are made many of which form a basis for job selection and job finding later on. Careers teachers rightly object to one or two glamorous visits which prevent any balanced judgment-forming even if they are worked out in detail. They advocate either none or many. Teachers in constructing their curricula are remarkably free from economic pressures and in the inner city in particular there is seldom any domination by a single industry. The trouble lies the other way: that teachers have difficulty in grasping the complexity of the opportunities so as to be able to give help when help is most needed. Peter Willmott, describing Bethnal Green in the late 1950s, provides a table showing the geographical spread of adolescent workers from Bethnal Green according to type of work (*Adolescent Boys of East London*, Penguin Books, 1966).

Adolescents Living in Bethnal Green

	Non-manual (%)	Skilled (%)	Semi and unskilled (%)
East End	29	60	49
City and central London	65	32	41
Elsewhere	6	8	10
	100	100	100

The investigation which needs to be made is into the way the 41 per cent of less skilled boys found their jobs in the City and central London. Relatives give important help to youngsters about finding their way through the maze of central London. It is not clear what happens to those who have neither effective relations nor the confidence to use official agencies. The school may have a new role to play with the help of the Youth Employment Service. The vacuum created by the breakdown of family bonds and of the assumption that there is always some official agency to deal with the sufferers is the barely recognised phenomenon to which the school might pay attention. The substantial investigation for the Central Youth Employment Executive gets bogged down by the complexities of the task and might have been more helpful if it had been confined to those failing to qualify for apprenticeships in inner city schools (R. Thomas and D. Wetherell, *Looking Forward to Work*, HMSO, 1974). For this manageable number, schemes providing work experience could be established.

Work experience is now permissible in the last year of schooling and typically it offers for each pupil two or three fortnights attached to a work-place helping and being helped to fit into new surroundings. The preparatory work may include visits by foremen to the school to explain their point of view and the teachers may ask the pupils to bring back some information about the firm which can be used in school lessons. As yet the outcome of work experience schemes has not been adequately written up and there is always a fear that the trade unions may oppose any widespread development of them.

Moreover, as unemployment increases there are fewer employers keen to attract additional workers. This lack of written material is unfortunate, leading to good ideas about briefing, selection of jobs and methods of follow-up lying dormant. It is said that it is difficult to stimulate fruitful discussions because the pupils cannot envisage the work situations of each other. Nevertheless the interest in jobs is great and is capable of supporting a long series of lessons even when many have already decided which jobs they are going to choose.

In order to place the fifteen-year-olds in suitable work-places and supervise them adequately so that they find the experience thought-provoking rather than boring, it is necessary to provide more staff than is usually allotted to the early leavers. A school attains prestige by the achievements of its best pupils and there is little incentive to equate expenditure for the final years of those who leave early and those who leave late. Some children never have the experiences which can be provided when class sizes are small. Looked at another way those children who are neglected at home are often those on whom least is spent at school – unless they become delinquent. In later life they swell the ranks of those who are frequently out of work. A little money spent wisely at the right time could be an economy in the long run.

Work experience fits very easily into the framework of a community school. I do not mean community *centre* schools which are no more than a copy of the Village Colleges of Cambridgeshire. These schools do a little more than make double use of their buildings since they set out to provide so-called permanent education for those who want it. However the community *service* schools are quite different from these since they aim to give and receive help from people and firms in their catchment area so as to build up an educative environment, a place where it is an education just to grow up. The community educators exemplified a workable form of deschooling long before Illich was known. It is characteristic of community schools that they study the needs of their areas whether these seem to be the gap between education and the job market, or accident blackspots or an absence of community feeling. Then the curriculum is adjusted accordingly so that the needs can be met.

It is hard to decide whether any existing schools in Britain match up to this description but, since the first account of them on television in 1955, a body of articles and books has been written (A. N. Gillett, 'Where the school is the centre of the community', in K. Gibberd, *Your Teenage Children*, Macdonald, 1964). There is no question that if such schools develop and spread from their promising beginnings a major contribution will be made to closing the gap between school and work. The very fact that children will learn their way around in a complex society ensures that they will be more adept at finding a suitable job and filling it adequately.

Work experience and community schools demand teachers with a new kind of training and experience. It is argued by some that teachers are incapable of doing more than they are doing at present. This appears convincing at first glance, but teachers are capable in some countries and find satisfaction in undertaking a significant and 'relevant' job. Job satisfaction for teachers is of importance; in the inner city schools they seldom gain much satisfaction from examination results, the more they are disappointed by the attitude of children and parents to their subjects the more appropriate it becomes to look to community development as a means of satisfaction. The experience of the EPAs reported by Halsey points to the value of schools enjoying a two-way relationship with their social and physical environment. Such community schools are strongly recommended in the report, but the difficult task of finding suitable teachers is not stressed. Work experience for teachers during their initial or in-service training undoubtedly helps, but in operating such schemes the teachers who are most at home in firm or factory bring back disappointing reports. Everything has been so familiar to them that they have failed to notice what is under their noses, ranging from the date on an old machine to a remark suitable for setting off a discussion on right and wrong. In short, work experience by itself without any discussion or guidance is not enough.

Further, teachers might be helped by undertaking social work, gaining a knowledge of the social services and meeting those city councillors who have an overall view of the city's needs.

An encyclopaedic knowledge of the school's area and the appropriate affection for it might be promoted if every school built up loose-leaf records not merely under subject headings but including the results of opinion surveys, lists of people able and willing to act as resource people on account of unusual skills, journeys or other experiences. It is possible to envisage a familiarity with the local job market forming part of local social studies – an essential core subject for all. It is not that the locality is studied in isolation but in comparison with other places, so the teachers need practice in making these kinds of comparisons and in drawing out resource people to obtain the full value of their visit. The teacher has to show the same confidence in working with all sorts of people that he expects of the pupils when they leave school. Learning by imitation in these circumstances is one of the best ways to learn, but it demands versatility and it demands incentives for teachers and pupils in the form of examinations and sixth-form study which do not exist at present.

It would be hard to end without mentioning the special difficulties of coloured people in obtaining jobs. The difficulties seem to be a matter of degree rather than fundamentally different. If there is no employer with whom they have something in common it points to the importance of encouraging the rise of employers in each minority group. If many leavers obtain their jobs through relatives and such links are lacking for a minority group this is where help must be concentrated.

Bernstein's writing draws attention to the failure to communicate between people who use the same language but use it differently, because language is inevitably related to past experience. This brake on such social processes as finding jobs is more serious for minority groups.

Assuming that the analysis is right the implications are clear. They include the selection and training of teachers to be able to adapt to school leavers without qualifications on the one hand, and to employers on the other, and who can organise work experience schemes within a framework of community education without damaging their career prospects.

A number of contributors continued the discussion of initiatives. David Eversley reiterated that the educational system is still very poorly linked to a rapidly changing urban economy. His views were supported by John Bazalgette. David Eversley then went on to look at the extent of the mismatch between school leavers' skills and the kinds of jobs that are available. A further illustration of this mismatch comes from the evidence provided by Patricia Haikin. Considerable numbers of 16 + adolescents are moving into further education because they are so ill equipped to begin work.

(b) Need for better links between school and work – 1 *David Eversley*

Since the first conference, education as a preparation for life has become an even dirtier phrase than it was then. Education has increasingly become concerned with values and visual appreciation and feeling. This is all right, but it does not help children obtain the kind of jobs which will enable them to lead the life style I want them to lead. I know this is a minority view. But it is a radical demand that a child should be prepared for the kind of life where he can take his place in the world as it is, and not in a world about which many people dream.

What is the mismatch in the urban employment market? As I tried to show earlier (pp. 28–30) in London, Manchester, Liverpool and all the big cities there is a grave shortage of manpower to take the sort of jobs the city does offer which are extremely well paid, which have career prospects and which enable people to make choices about their lives. The mismatch is between the higher, more prestigious jobs on the one hand, and most of the labour which is on offer on the other.

Why do children make the wrong choice at the age of sixteen? Part of the reason is the family pressure for some poor children to obtain almost any work so as to add to the family's finances. In order to combat this we ought to be considering a system of generous cash allowances for those children from poor homes who stay on at school beyond the minimum leaving age. But part of the reason for the 'bad' choices of employment is to be found within the schools themselves. The curricula of most secondary schools are dangerously outdated. Hordes of youngsters from inner city schools are pushed on to the labour market with skills that limit them to dead-end employment. As soon as these children have married and begun their own families they are plunged into what Rowntree described as primary poverty.

I do not believe that these children are ineducable. I believe they are capable of acquiring the skills and qualifications which will enable them to take the better-paid jobs and stay in the inner city. As a matter of urgency the government ought to consider making the curricula of our secondary schools more relevant to the local labour market in which the schools are situated.

(c) Need for better links between school and work – 2 *John Bazalgette*

What are the particular areas of urban change about which educators need to know in order to be able to equip the rising generation to move successfully into a rapidly changing world? One of the areas upon which I think we have not yet touched is the current impact of economic and technological change. I stress this as being significant because some work that the Grubb Institute has been doing on the transition from school to work indicates that the kind of assumptions and models to which teachers work are based on a perception of the world outside more relevant to Victorian industrialism than the inner city of today. And when young people leave school they discover something totally different, with the consequence that they reject all their school experience.

We not only need to equip the teachers to be able to understand the family/community situation of young people. We must also help the teachers to understand the employment system. One of the greatest weaknesses at the moment is the detachment of teachers and educators from the changes in economic and technological structures. These are changing very fast, and one of the things that they are losing as they change is any conception about human development.

Employers and managers are desperately worried about the effects of this upon young workers. They certainly do not come and talk to teachers because of the entrenched hostility between the educational system and the employment system. The only people who are tackling that hostility are the children, as they leave one group for the other. They are therefore in danger of becoming the victims of both the lack of humanity at the work-place and the conflict between schools and employment.

(d) Need for better links between school and work – 3 *Patricia Haikin*

One of the distinct areas of need that we notice in further education is youngsters who have left school unprepared for what they have to cope with. There is no obvious agency responsible for this group, and this need. Some of these youngsters flock into further education, but do not at present get a very good deal here either. They say: 'I am not ready to work; I do not want to work; I wish to continue the thing that is called education.' Most further education colleges keep them for two years, or even more. The students have a specific vocational need. They need counselling; they need support; they need something maybe along the lines of the government work schemes that have just appeared. But there is nothing in the structure at the moment to work with disaffected, unsure youngsters of this age group. They will not go back to their schools. They come into a further education system which imperfectly understands their problems, and is at the moment in no way geared to meet these problems.

Peter Newell begins our discussion on alternative patterns of education by looking at the educational crisis which authorities refuse to face. He

*sees the symptoms of this crisis in increasing apathy and disorder
within the schools, falling standards, increasing truancy by both pupils
and teachers, and high teacher turnover. Peter Newell believes that a
more constructive debate on educational reform will follow the asking
of the right basic questions. We should be asking ourselves what are the
aims of learning, and what resources do people need for learning now?
These questions have been asked and partly answered at the White
Lion Street free school in Islington.*

3 Alternative patterns of education

(a) The free school in Islington *Peter Newell*

We need to start from the question 'What resources do people
need for learning now?'. Instead, the debate almost always starts
from 'How can we repair the present school system?'; or, less
defensively, 'How can we get more people to take advantage of this
great system we have built up?'. That sort of pseudo-question
arises from a fear of radical institutional change, and from the
continuing confusion of schooling with education.

For some time now the defence of gradual reform rather than
radical restructuring of the mainstream education system has been
wearing a little thin. There has been the great (and highly profitable
for some) boom in curriculum reform and new gadgetry; more and
more glossy packaging of 'educational' parcels; the labelling of
increasingly large proportions of the school population as maladjusted or deviant in one way or another, and research project
after research project (the deprivation industry – recycling deprivation for its own ends) confirming over and over again facts which
were commonplace to anyone really in touch with urban family
life.

Meanwhile local authorities were preoccupied with what seemed
(still seems apparently) to some of them to be 'the last great reform' –
comprehensive reorganisation. But the removal of the 11 plus,
while it is a welcome relief from a particularly vicious form of
selection, is not a prescription for any particular pattern of education.
It is in that sense a negative reform. In the rush to provide the
greatest possible range of examination courses in the name of
equality of opportunity, the possibility of alternative patterns to
that of the large school never really surfaced. It has taken a long
time to become apparent that real choice is not synonymous with
the proliferation of entirely artificial 'options' between one imposed
curriculum package and another.

Faced with a growing resentment from pupils against the imposed pattern (resentment can show itself in apathy as well as action), the authorities spend an increasing amount of time plastering over cracks and pretending nothing is wrong in case it upsets their own and their teachers' morale still further.

The consumers increasingly opt out by truanting, placing their parents in an illegal situation. At the same time the authorities find it increasingly difficult to cope with teacher turnover, and put themselves outside the law by condoning part-time schooling, prolonged suspensions, etc.

And now they have also somehow to explain away the apparent worsening of general standards of literacy and numeracy. To blame *this* on the children and their parents might suggest that learning was an expression of individual will – and where would that belief lead the present school system?

The teacher unions took advantage of the temporary glut of resources of the 1960s, and leapt on the professional bandwagon. As in other professions, there is a great deal of self-interest which is not compatible with the enabling role that is in the interests of the majority of learners. Just as in medicine the profession has imposed an emphasis on treatment rather than prevention, so in education the teaching profession has emphasised professional authority at the expense of individual autonomy.

And only professional self-interest can explain some of the more glaring illogicalities of the education system we have – for example the concentration of resources on those who least need them, the irony of a teacher–pupil ratio at postgraduate level often of 1 to 1, and at primary level of 1 to 30 or less. And as for nursery education. . . .

The importing of American anti-schooling literature, and South American trained de-schooling theorists have provided a new and fashionable academic distraction, and certainly broadened for a time quite a few arguments amongst the 'professionals'. All words. No, or very few, prescriptions for action now. The questions raised did provoke over-reaction from some predictable quarters – the then NUT general secretary spluttered about 'educational quislings', revealing after his speech that he hadn't even read much of the literature first.

The vested interests of so many in the education system make them conscious or unconscious opponents of anything that goes beyond tinkering with the system we have. Within the state system, anything that looks remotely different from the conventional school is only acceptable if it is limited to some labelled group of children, and used to 'rehabilitate' them in some way and get them back into 'proper' schools as quickly as possible. More of that trend later.

Take one prominent example of this refusal to ask basic questions, and find radical solutions: more or less everyone accepts that one of the great obstacles to learning in schools is the ratio of adults to children. Everyone must also by now be able to see that it is quite impractical to think of removing the obstacle by training more vast armies of professionals (in fact we are training fewer it seems). Only a radical change in the use of manpower resources, a removal of bogus professionalisms and fragmented roles can really change things – and that of course is unthinkable.

So the system still goes lumbering on, with so much institutional momentum and increasingly centralised control that it becomes further and further removed from the real interests of its consumers. Tinkering is not going to change its direction. Only basic questioning can do that.

What resources do people need for learning now? What are the aims of learning? If learning is seen as an expression of individual will, and if its aim is seen as maximising individual choice, and people's control over their own lives, then no specific institutional model is going to come up as the solution. Choice and control are not things that can be imposed on others – on the contrary, imposition limits choice and removes control.

A look at most schools – and particularly of course secondary schools – in the light of these sorts of questions and general aims immediately reveals all sorts of constraints that limit and inhibit learning. What have pre-packaged curricula, external examinations, petty rules and regulations, school uniforms, corporal punishment and other punishment systems, compulsory timetables, rigid staff hierarchies, compulsory religious instruction, limited periods of study, terms and holidays, limited age groups, centralised bureaucratic controls, compulsory attendance got to do with increasing individuals' choice and control?

Tinkering with the content of learning within the context of these sorts of constraint has about as much effect on the end product as changing the menu would have in a long-stay prison. (Of course all this has not been lost on all those tinkering curriculum reformers. Efforts like the Schools Council's social education and moral education projects soon got round to producing materials intended oh-so-tactfully to change the power structure in the classroom, or even in the school. A recipe for schizophrenia for all involved.)

The demolition job on the existing school system and the analysis of its real effects has been done frequently and at great length elsewhere. A number of education departments seem to spend a great deal of energy promoting it, without recognising the apparent illogicality of their own situation. The demolition is seldom accompanied by any sort of prescription for action now. It is easy to be defeatist and merely confirm that schools by themselves have very little effect. They are of course reflections of inequality branded deep in society, but in their role as a sorting process they do in fact have a most powerful negative effect on the vast majority who do not succeed in their terms. By paying lip-service to the concept of equality of opportunity, they make the failure of this majority seem somehow legitimate. They reinforce the feelings of helplessness, apathy, lack of responsibility. Why else should standards of basic literacy and numeracy continue to fall in many areas, despite ever-increasing periods of schooling, more and more tinkering?

What are the alternatives? One, of course, is to preach demolition, to hold seminars on the alternative society, or schools without walls, in the hope that some time that society will mysteriously appear, or all the walls will fall down. It's a comfortable alternative but an unrealistic one, a make-believe world of words and hopes.

Another alternative is the one we in Islington and some others here are engaged in, and of course the one which we regard as having most hope and relevance at the moment. It is to use the surprisingly flexible law on education to create an institutional model free as far as possible from the constraints that separate school from learning: to provide an enabling institution with the general aim of maximising the individual's choice and control. We are working, of course, within the context of an extremely unjust and unequal society, and that means that today's model may not suit tomorrow. For instance, theorising about the degree of community control that is possible now is pointless. There can be no general prescription, no central solution. (A favourite tactic of those inherently opposed to fundamental structural changes is to take a concept like community control to its logical extreme, and then challenge the exponents of the concept to explain why in a particular situation it has not yet been fully adopted.)

We have to acknowledge that as enablers we walk a tightrope between paternalism and laissez-faire. As pedlars of an alternative that is so very different from the accepted and conventional model of school, we are also open to all sorts of pressures which have nothing to do with the rightness or wrongness of the model for its own local consumers (shortage of money and struggle for physical survival, endless visitors and publicity).

To a great degree, the definition of our model can only be negative – in terms of the removal of inhibiting constraints to learning in the conventional school. Some of it is easy enough – no staff hierarchy; a sharing of job-roles such as cooking, cleaning, accounting, maintenance, etc.; a structure of meetings for formal decision-making; no generalised curriculum; no compulsory timetable or compulsory learning activities; no imposed rules or regulations (except in the case of very young children); the removal of age barriers on learning activities; flexibility of attendance through longer opening hours and shorter holidays; no attempt to bring education into the building – it is used as a base for exploration of educational resources outside it.

Much of this is only possible with a very small institution, one in which communication can be immediate, and in which size does not breed its own authority. The flexibility which is essential if people are to use the centre to meet their own needs is incompatible with large size. The other overpowering reason for smallness is accessibility.

Another all-important part of the 'negative' definition is that the institution should not be defined as 'educational'. The street centre (which in our area seems the most appropriate and least loaded name) can be a sharing point for all kinds of community resources not conventionally interpreted as 'educational'; for entertainment, for the borrowing of equipment, for meetings, for shared transport, food-buying, printing facilities, etc., etc. Of course, if 'educational' meant, as it might again some day, merely 'encouraging the growth of human horizons', then the description could stand. But now that education is so much confused with schooling, it cannot.

It cannot, for example, comfortably be called educational, these days, to lend our saucepans or even spanners, to show funny films, provide meals and chat. But these may indeed be just what people need to enable them to expand their horizons. Why should we demand an institutionalised separation of such needs from book learning? Those who do want to make the separation all too easily forget that they themselves probably have both. And the economic structure which gave them both is precisely that which deprives most people of the luxury.

Is the definition of this type of institution totally negative? No, because the aim of increasing individual choice and control is as basic as you can get, and has very many positive implications in individual relationships and situations. Given a society suffering from years of oppression and an acute lack of individual control for most people (and schooling stereotypes which have made a deep impression on all who have come into contact with them), a simple vacuum of 'freedom', a removal of all outside initiatives would not be an enabling exercise. It would be about as artificial and disconnected from real life at this stage as are most conventional schools. Removing the constraints that inhibit learning in schools does not imply devaluing learning. It is perfectly possible to generalise about certain tools which are essential for autonomy given the sort of society we all live in: a command of reading and writing and talking, ability to research rather than retain information, decision-making based on sifting of information and discussion. But our encouragement of the development of these skills in adults and children is done within the context of no compulsion. The other justification of our initiatives is that the choice of learning activities which we help to provide (apart from the ever-present choice of doing 'nothing') is based on a very close and continuing knowledge of the whole-life context of the individuals concerned; a knowledge that the smallness of the centre and its closeness to their homes makes possible.

This, then, is the basic unit for a new and alternative pattern: the small, multi-purpose all-age street centre, accountable to its local community, financed centrally on a per capita basis. Given the present monopoly of learning resources in the schooled system, it is going to require considerable initiative and expertise to shift resources from schooling to learning. It is not money that is needed, nor is it the type of professional training that is used only to mystify, and to justify differentials of pay and esteem. Some training is certainly needed – teaching reading for example requires an understanding of some concepts which could take more than a week or two to pass on. But the main requirement for enablers is a belief in the aim of maximising individuals' choice and control, and a conviction that it is this aim which should dominate their role in other people's learning.

These small, basic units, which must be regarded as bases, not total institutions, do of course need to be serviced by other specialist resources. As bases, they require access to specialist skills and specialist equipment. Libraries and sports centres already exist, but of course at present the pyramid of educational provision is absolutely the wrong way up – we spend most on the facilities to which access is most limited. No wonder resources appear stretched when there is such duplication and such incredible lavishness at one end of the spectrum.

How can this sort of pattern develop from where we are now? One-off centres like ours have to be given a sufficient lease of life to convince local authorities that it is their duty to support us centrally without the control that they are used to. That precedent once established becomes of use to other local centres. Each existing educational institution has to be persuaded to ask itself basic questions about the sort of resources for learning that are needed, and by whom, and the real contribution towards meeting those needs that can be made. Somewhere, a local education authority has to take the plunge and provide for the development in an area of a new pattern of street centres and specialist resources.

London, like many cities, has a perfect opportunity for this kind of experiment now, because of the falling inner city population and falling rolls that threaten to close many schools and make a lot of capital resources redundant unless smallness becomes respectable again (and we don't mean schools for 750). The ILEA would need to take a small area – say a square mile – arrange for a survey of all its resources (i.e. not just conventional educational ones), and open a debate with all local organisations and groups on the feasibility of a decentralised and radically different pattern, with information available for all on the resources both capital and revenue at present used for that population. And above all, with the expectation that the authority's role in the development of the new pattern would be that of servicing, advising and financing, not policy-making.

There is an apparent contradiction here: would not the authority be imposing small units in just the same way as at the moment it imposes large purpose-built comprehensives wherever it gets the chance and the money? The difference is similar to the difference between enabling and imposition in the role of the teacher. The small units would enable people to take control over their learning and many other facets of their lives; whereas the large units must impose a structure which limits choice and removes control.

It is very hard to see what an authority like the ILEA has to lose by such action, and yet they have spent almost a year now, still with no conclusion, trying to decide whether or not they should join Islington Borough Council in funding the White Lion Street free school. (*Editor's note:* in March 1975 the ILEA turned down the school's application for support. The school is re-applying.) This may well be more to do with the ponderous nature of their decision-making process than with the significance of the precedent they may or may not set.

Their energies at the moment go into funding pseudo-alternatives within the existing structure – even, most absurd, within the existing schools. Nurture groups, intermediate treatment centres, truancy projects, special difficulties funds; all aim at propping up the mainstream system by labelling and parcelling off growing hordes of disaffected consumers. Schools – 'proper' schools that is – have so much to offer that nothing must be done which might suggest that their pattern was not the only possible pattern. The moment any of these special units begins to really prosper, its autonomy is seen as a threat to the rationale of the big unit (which of course it is), and conflict sets in – there are plenty of examples in London now. People working in the small units for any length of time see that the real needs and interests of their consumers can only be met when they are able to express their autonomy.

If Philadelphia can finance projects like Parkway, Melbourne can finance small autonomous community schools alongside its high schools, Alum Rock and other places can experiment with weighted voucher schemes aimed at encouraging a divergence of educational provision and so on, why cannot some British urban authority just try a different pattern?

Some suggest that this would be sacrificing some children like guinea-pigs for the sake of experiment. At present, it is the vast majority whose learning is sacrificed in a huge compulsory and expanding laboratory called the school system.

(b) The free school in Barrowfield *John Macbeath*

Peter Newell has just referred to the view held by many LEAs that a unit of 750 is a small school. In Barrowfield Community School in Glasgow it was felt that a unit of 40 might well be too large. There is obviously no prescriptive size for schools, but my own feeling is that the optimum size is reached at the point where it is still unnecessary to introduce structures and strictures to order people's relationships to one another. Size becomes dysfunctional to the aims of education when human relationships are replaced by bureaucratic ones, and identities become concealed behind badges, letters, numbers and rank orders.

In Barrowfield we felt that the unit should be small enough not to allow more open scrutiny and control but to facilitate a more open development of relationships. To some observers, it appeared that herein lay the long-sought-after panacea to the problems of schooling. Not after all programmed learning, educational television, curriculum development or a computer terminal in every school, but *size* – the key to a successful unit was apparently to keep it small. At this period there were actually only ten pupils in the school, and coincidentally a number of Scottish education authorities started to talk about alternatives to the large comprehensive based on a unit of ten.

Some of these 'alternatives' are now in operation. Ostensibly for those who find it less congenial in the large impersonal environment of the comprehensive these units provide a more intimate pastoral contact. Predictably those who end up there are not self-selected, but those who from the teachers' or administrators' view are most urgently in need of an alternative. The implicit aim of the alternative is a cooling-out process whereby the most institutionally misshapen might be re-formed and recycled eventually to take up their place again in the normal order.

Some parents whose children have wound up in these units have not surprisingly felt that this was no alternative at all, but a halfway house to or substitute for an approved school. Since neither parent nor pupil was involved in the choice of alternative it is hard to deny their perceptions. Here was the essential difference between these 'alternatives' and the alternative of Barrowfield Community School. The constant succession of visitors came with the question 'What can I learn to take back to my own school?' but the crucial aspect of Barrowfield was one that could not be transplanted. It was not merely the size, but that it came into being through the initiative of the parents, and could only continue to survive through their interest and enthusiasm.

At least one local head simply refused to believe that in this kind of area there was enough initiative or reservoir of discontent among parents to make them start their own school. It could only be a diabolical ploy of unsuccessful or subversive trendies seducing children and parents away from the benevolent despotism of his own institution. In fact, though, a group of concerned parents did get together in 1972 and made an approach to the College of Education to request help and advice in setting up their own school as had been done in Liverpool. From that overture came months of discussion among the parents, future teachers and prospective pupils, and from that dialogue was born a genuine community school with its roots firmly in the groundbed of the local area, its traditions and its real (not merely perceived) needs.

Legally and practically the school belongs to the parents and the pupils. It is in fact and theory their school and they may do what they like with it. Is it surprising that they do not wreck the furniture, break the windows or destroy the equipment? Indeed if this does happen, as for example when a group of extra-territorials broke in and sprayed graffiti on the walls, the kids were upset, even outraged. They are genuinely proud of their school, as exemplified when television or newspaper articles appear to them unfair, and they write in protest to the editor. Yet nobody has ever tried to convince them that this is their school, to be proud of it, to keep up its good name, etc. Such sloganising can only be a deceit where the reality is quite at odds with the mythology. This school feels and is undeniably their own.

The problem is not immediately so with the next generation. At the end of the first year six of the ten original pupils had reached the age of sixteen, and their parents, in accordance with a wholly unshakeable tradition, took them out of school and put them to work. This meant a new intake who had not physically or morally built the school, who would find a pre-existing structure which was not theirs but somebody else's. This posed a real question – should the school be in a sense destroyed, and re-created the following year? It would have been a bizarre thing to do, perhaps, but it did reflect a concern for the creative involvement of the newcomers. Although the new kids did in the end have to accommodate to something ongoing, they brought a new set of attitudes, or more correctly, a whole new individuality, and the character of the school changed in accordance with that. This seemed a sign, at least, that the school was still alive.

Our discussion continues by concentrating on the role of parents in alternative forms of education. John Macbeath suggests that parents should use teachers partly as technicians; in other words as people who can suggest practical ways of running educational establishments. But Peter Newsam in his contribution suggests that parents may well ask for reactionary reforms. Such a view is countered by Virginia Makins, who gently chides Peter Newsam for his administrator's paranoia. Joe Rogaly brings this part of the discussion to a conclusion with the description of the Danish 'Lille-school' experiment.

4 Parents and alternative patterns of education

(a) Using the teachers' expertise *John Macbeath*

Parents about to start their own school quite understandably, as in the case of Barrowfield, turn to the obvious professional sources for help. If they had decided to run it themselves they would probably have settled for the very traditional *modus operandi* they had been familiar with as pupils. The 'professionals' who agreed to be involved saw themselves as offering alternative suggestions, but accepting that in the end the operation of the school would have to be based on a consensus of parental wishes, as well as the expressed wishes of pupils and teachers.

To reach such an end point required opening a dialogue in which different parties could argue for certain ideas, be won over on some issues, compromise on others, and refuse to compromise where essential principles were involved. This was a long and rather messy process, but it was a dialogue in that it involved the education of all, 'teachers' as well as parents and pupils. The pupils, who at this stage of the proceedings were rather overwhelmed and indeed less interested, have since made a much more important contribution in the day-to-day running of the school where, if a suggested activity does not meet with their approval, they are free to propose alternatives and win converts to their project. The essential point to reiterate is that made by Peter Newell: it is a self-educating community where demarcations between teachers and learners are blurred, if not eradicated, and where the expertise of teachers is neither denied nor invested with mystique and magic.

(b) Requesting reactionary reforms *Peter Newsam*

I see one danger in letting parents decide the kind of educational experiments to be conducted. The most impressively dreary educational occurrence I have met in London derived from a group of parents who set up a 'school' where they had the children sitting in rows, for spelling lessons all day long. It represented nearly everything that this conference would detest, but was firmly backed by a particular group of parents.

How is the bureaucracy to react to this? On what grounds, if any, are we to bless one experiment while officially frowning on another? This is the question you must consider if you are going to ask educational authorities to provide support for independent initiatives.

(c) Administrator's paranoia *Virginia Makins*

I should like to follow on from Peter Newsam's last remarks. He seems to be showing surprising signs of what you might call administrator's paranoia: 'My God, they are all going to want it and then what are we going to do?' It seems to me highly unlikely that very many parents are going to put in effort of the kind required to establish a free school. And even if some of these parents want to establish what some people might regard as an old-fashioned school, can that really be considered a disaster when you think what is happening in many of our secondary schools at the moment? I believe it is important to encourage a number of different experiments and that these should be financed through central funds. I should very much support the idea of the 'Danish little school' approach which Joe Rogaly advocates in the following section.

(d) Danish Lille-schools *Joe Rogaly*

In Denmark any group can start a school, and provided that it meets certain criteria the government will meet 80 per cent of its costs. The criteria are very broad – the school must follow the same curriculum as state schools, giving the same number of hours of education per week and so on. Using this law a number of 'Lille' or little schools, with between 50 and 150 pupils each, have been founded. This movement began in 1949 in a wave of reaction against large state schools that at that time practised rigid old-fashioned methods of teaching. The Lille-schools followed the then most advanced English notions of progressive education. Today there are about 40 or more of them and many are Marxist in orientation, the parents who founded them being that way inclined. The same law has also facilitated the founding of other more traditional types of publicly subsidised but privately managed school, mostly to meet the needs of religious groups.

In the following section we consider the role teachers should and can play in educational experiments. Peter Newell argues that the extent of positive choice in schools is going to depend very much on the initiatives taken by adults within the schools. John Macbeath gives a practical example of how students at the Barrowfield Free School help to determine their own curriculum. Peter Newell looks at the extent of student control over the school's expenditure and expulsion from the Islington Free School, and the role of examination. Eric Midwinter then discusses the lessons he draws from the Liverpool EPA project. In doing so he looks at what is meant by a community school and then goes on to stress the importance of survival of recent experiments.

5 Inside the free school

(a) Role of teachers *Peter Newell*

John Bazalgette: I want to ask two questions. First, what distinct contributions do adults make to the free school? Second, what are the constraints on the free school?

Peter Newell: I think there is a group of free schoolers who believe that all initiatives should come and will come from the children, and that the adult role is a totally submissive one. I do not share this view. Children are not going to develop autonomy in a situation in which the adults cannot be autonomous. As adults we have gained skills and knowledge which are worth passing on. The degree of real choice in an institution is going to be very much the responsibility of the adults within it, and the offers that they make. This does not have to imply any compulsion, but if the learning activities offered are going to be effective, it does imply a lot of planning and structure.

The obvious external constraints on the free school are current educational law (the attendance regulations, etc., which are open to very flexible interpretation) and other legal frameworks. Until local authorities recognise that these new model institutions should be encouraged, at least on an experimental basis, by per capita finance, shortage of money remains another constraint.

(b) Students choosing their own curriculum *John Macbeath*

It would seem an obvious principle that pupils should be given choice as to what they themselves are going to be responsible for studying. But the ideal choice is constrained by the adults who have to accommodate to decisions made, and by one's past experience too. Both in Barrowfield and in other projects involving the school's failures, I have observed a stereotypical reaction from children offered a complete range of free choice – an opting for such mythical entities as 'geography' or 'English'. Imagine sitting down with an adolescent of fourteen and asking him what of all things he would like to do that most interests him and being met with 'English' as a response.' When pressed it transpires that English represents an association with a place or person where activities were less painful, sometimes even enjoyable, but what those activities were or meant is long forgotten. When faced with choice in an apparently 'educational' context it is natural to have recourse to some points of reference in school experience. But the real tragedy (it is not too strong a word) that faces children in situations like Barrowfield is that they have never had, in school or elsewhere, the opportunity to exercise any kind of real choice, and to give them a choice of school subjects or projects and the illusion of freedom may be an empty liberal gesture. Nevertheless there seems no better principle than that of respecting the rights of individuals to choose and refuse, and having accepted this it becomes incumbent on the teacher to persuade and convince in those areas where he thinks he knows best, but ultimately to accept the freedom of the child to reject what is patently 'best' for him.

(c) Control of expenditure and expulsions *Peter Newell*

John Bazalgette: Do they have any control over what you get paid? I am in touch with a youth club where the members sign the salary cheques and the whole question about controlling the expenditure, including the payment of the salaries, is one of the most important educational processes in which these young children are involved.

Peter Newell: In the free school in Islington the pupils have control over a great deal of the expenditure. They could have control over what we are paid. The fact is that they have not asked for this. We have meetings open to children, parents and workers, during which we plan the school's expenditure and everyone is encouraged to attend. The only subjects which are not discussed in a full meeting with parents and children are individual children or families, or deciding which children should come to the school. I do not know if this is sensible or not; it is certainly arbitrary. But we have explained the reasons, and as yet there is no opposition.

(d) Expanding the need for qualifications *Peter Newell*

I should like to say more about the question of exams. This is one which is often raised when the discussion turns to the free schools. We are concerned about increasing individuals' choice and control over their own lives, so it would seem extraordinary to me not to explain to the children how society works at the moment, what exams do for people and what sort of chances are widened by qualifications and what are not. At the same time I think we should also explain that the children should not think of exams as a judgment of their personal worth, nor should they become neurotic about them. At the free school in Islington we do not see anything incompatible in the fact that a number of our children want to take O levels. Whether they will or not I do not know – many of the older ones have been convinced by previous schools' attitudes that the exam world is not for them.

(e) Securing the future of educational experiments *Eric Midwinter*

What might broadly be termed the 'community development' movement forms a mainstream reaction to the problems loosely grouped as the 'urban crisis'. It is dually motivated. There is the moral view about the need for a more socially just society, together with the pragmatic belief that, unless society is radically reformed, it could become critically unstable. The general principles concentrate both on a more egalitarian distribution of resources and facilities and a more democratic or 'participatory' infrastructure so that people might involve themselves more positively.

The educational component of this movement is normally concerned with 'community schooling', by which is meant a school that draws its life-blood from the catchment community and, one hopes, helps children and adults to make a more critical and compassionate contribution to that community's improving stature and quality. It recognises that education, like other social elements, is a dimension of everyone's lives, not just that brief academic introduction of childhood. It recognises that the totality of everyone's experience forms an 'educative community', mobile, shifting and dynamic, which at any given moment importantly dictates educational attainment. Alternatively, it is hopeful that, through a curriculum substance and method more closely related to the children's actual life-style, the school might service the community's attempts, in A. H. Halsey's phrase, 'to raise the heights of its dilemmas'. It draws, obviously, on the traditions of community schools. These have conventionally dealt with the more fruitful use of plant, with schools open for adult use in evenings or at weekends; and, especially in primary schools, a more generous view of teacher–parent relations; and the tendency to imbue the curriculum with a more relevant character. Up and down the country pioneer modes have been colourfully attempted in areas normally associated with 'urban crisis', and one is now able to tease out new approaches to home–school relations and curriculum which are appropriate to the urban culture. It is worth stressing that this is no more (and no less) than the application of a general principle to a particular cultural typology during a particular epoch. It illustrates an important point that education (as well as the other elements on the socio-economic gamut) should not be singular or uniform in character. It should be carefully organised and monitored to fit as snugly as possible into the immediate situation – this is the 'local diagnosis' recommended by the Halsey Report.

Of course, by initially accepting the prior influence of home and background rather than school vis-à-vis educational advance, it goes without saying that, however well reformed the school, it could never take up that position of effective dictation of events which its more optimistic protagonists once visualised. However, given any move towards a more socially just and 'participatory' society, it would be necessary to ensure that an education service existed which could underpin and maybe accelerate that move. It is not a case either of society creating the school or vice versa: this is a cyclic process, and the premise for the community school is the certainty of that interlock.

It is, needless to say, a frankly revisionist view, whereby one hopes both to maintain and improve society at one and the same time. The first instinct of the community school movement, as part of the community development movement, is to seek to work within the existing fabric. In regard to education, the enormous resources and personnel, to say nothing of the continuing virtues of the system, are sufficient reason for this practical, if humdrum, viewpoint. Unlike Peter Newell (see page 108) I do not believe we are talking about a wholly bad system, but one which shows several signs of being capable of radical alteration. This is why, in my opinion, it is essential first to float any pilot or innovatory activities within the public system, and second to ensure their survival.

One of the least helpful sets of attempts to resolve the urban crisis is that group of endeavours which have been attempted outside and in antagonism to the public sector. Apart from their short-term counter-productivity, they have, so to say, no visible means of support for the future. Even in the middle term, few large-scale implementations of a social kind are possible which are not public in finance and by control. The common denominator of survival and sustenance seems to rest in projects which are privately funded by foundation and trust or sponsored by governmental agencies, either way with the highest degree of local government co-operation. Some of the work begun by the EPA projects (1968–71) still survives precisely because of this. It began in partnership with local government and, where it seemed to be or demonstrated itself as 'good practice', it was taken permanently aboard by the local authority. The survival rate of EPA project activities is not over-impressive, but compared with the death (or suicide) rate of some other like endeavours, it has not been too gloomy, and what success there has been is largely due to a policy of political revisionism.

5
Conference Suggestions

The conference made a number of suggestions, and the most important of these are brought together in this final chapter. First Peter Newsam suggests that all those concerned with the inner city school should make the most of the fall in the school rolls. Peter Newell supports the plea that we should make the most of existing resources in the inner city area by taking a close look at the learning resources that people in the area need, and a re-structuring and redistribution in line with their needs. He stresses that 'learning resources' does not mean just the conventional educational institutions. Peter Newsam continues the dialogue by suggesting that we need to pay much more attention to why some schools succeed and others do not, and how we can spread success. This idea is then taken up by Eric Midwinter and John Macbeath. Peter Newsam returns to the forum to argue that many of the solutions to the problem of the inner city school lie within the educational sphere itself. This view is disputed by John Vaizey and Frank Field. Their plea is for greater emphasis on the need to attack the poverty of the inner city.

1 Making the most of falling numbers *Peter Newsam*

The fall in pupil numbers is crucial. In the inner cities of this country we have an opportunity which we may be failing to grasp imaginatively. Equally, we have a new set of problems to be solved. Take just a few examples of what is happening and is going to happen. The ratio of primary school teachers to secondary school teachers in our cities is going to change radically at least until births rise or outward migration is reversed. This will have incalculable effects. Another effect will be on the numbers and deployment of teachers. It will be difficult to get a job in a primary school in London next year. The arithmetic is simple. In one year you need 2,000 teachers and you get 2,200 coming forward. Suddenly you have 12,000 fewer children in primary schools and you need over 500 fewer teachers. So you have only 1,400 vacancies and still the same 2,200 people coming forward. And in the succeeding year, vacancies may be down by a further 500.

A further effect of falling numbers is that of costs. You do not achieve pro rata savings when numbers go down, and the inner cities are going to be landed with more than proportionate education costs.

Again, just at the very moment when people in inner cities are wanting to plan, they find that conditions under which planning can take place are disappearing. How far ought market forces to be allowed to operate? Just one example is the influence of parents when numbers fall. If a group of parents really want to, they will increasingly be able to close a primary school within a few weeks. There will be places in schools adjoining. The same may soon be true of secondary schools.

Education authorities will have to make their minds up on these matters. With falling numbers it is not sensible to try to plan supply, the quantity and quality of school places, while at the same time stimulating demand in the form of parental choice.

2 The square mile survey *Peter Newell*

I hesitate to suggest any form of research as being a useful way of spending money at present in inner cities, but we desperately need to know what learning and other community resources exist in the square mile around the White Lion Street free school in Islington. We also want to know if this plant is being used and if so, by whom. Once we have this information we can begin a real debate on the best use of resources. At present the debate is limited to tinkering with existing educational institutions: authorities do not know enough about the value of their resources, or about their real take-up.

3 How do we spread success? *Peter Newsam*

We should give more attention to the schools which succeed. How is it that some schools, judged in terms of the way in which the school operates as a community, the skills that the children acquire and the way in which they behave, are high performing schools, when all the indicators seem to suggest that they ought not to be so?

If there is one characteristic about these schools which seems to generate success, it appears to come from a group of teachers seeing themselves in some way as a group of people. Let me give you one startling example. It concerns a school with about the highest turnover of teachers in London. The staff were persuaded to go away for three or four days to think things over. In the process of thinking about what they were trying to do, in effect they resolved not to leave. They said 'let's stay put this year and see how things go'. The results of this decision on the school showed themselves in an enormous improvement in the quality of work and in the way in which children moved about the school. If I was asked to put my finger on what action was decisive in changing this school it was when that group of people said 'we as a group are going to take responsibility for the school and are going to make sure that it works'. The lesson I think we should read from this is that changes can be made, are made, and the problem for which one seeks a solution is how to transmit these forms of success.

4 Spreading news about success – 1 *Eric Midwinter*

One practical way of transmitting new and successful experiments in education would be to establish a training agency. Such an agency might be jointly financed by the private foundations and the local authorities. The LEAs would send teachers for what might be called induction courses, where they would be involved in the practical running of successful experiments.

The agency would recruit its students from the whole educational world. Its work ought to be relevant to educational visitors, home school teachers and college tutors, LEA advisers, head teachers and school governors and managers. It would attempt to dovetail coursework with workshop cum fieldwork exercises, thereby developing new training approaches as well as new roles. The overall important point is that the crucial agents in the possible reformation of the education system are the teachers. A full-scale effort in that direction is likely to be the most productive way of handling the issue. Pioneer experimentation in education of this kind could well be halted or slowed down for a spell; we run the risk of discovering the same bits and pieces over and over again. We really must consolidate the knowledge we have and screen it back through into the profession.

5 Spreading news about success – 2 *John Macbeath*

I have less optimism than Peter Newsam in the notion of answers lying within the education system, and am less sanguine than Eric

Midwinter about the universalisation of the small-scale project as a solution. One can agree with Peter Newsam that it is possible to visit schools and be impressed by the conspicuous absence of hierarchy, but in the regime we have in our schools it must be there, however well concealed, for accountability means accountability within a hierarchically ordered profession, and we have not as yet developed notions of accountability in other directions – to parents, to pupils, to communities.

Therefore, neither the extension of the best primary practice into secondaries, nor the extension of a successful free school at secondary level appears to me as solutions. For teachers in secondaries at the moment who do feel a genuine sense of accountability to their charges, it has to be translated into pressuring them against the inertia of their own choice to allow them if possible a clutch of CSEs or GCEs. Teachers in secondary schools who would genuinely like to change the plight of their pupils caught in an inner city trap find themselves ensnared in the curriculum–examination net.

But as far as change is concerned the most invidious aspect of this is that teachers have grown to love their oppressors, who in turn offer them a measure of security. So it is teachers themselves who come to represent the greatest obstacle to change. Teachers who work in the inner city and have an interest in maintaining or gently improving the system also see it as necessary to accept the realities of the situation, one of which is that the urban school has to be a reflection of the suburban school, for it must compete in the same system with the same parameters, the same expectations. This is the legacy of the comprehensive system, conceived not in the 1950s but in the nineteenth century, when it was decided that schooling should be for everybody and that it should be inextricably tied up with earning a living, economic status, power, influence, and ultimately with one's value as a human being. Teachers in this situation may come to terms with it in the way described by Nicholas Gillett, renouncing any pretence to equality of opportunity or equality of result, and attempting to find the match between pupils and jobs.

So as long as we are working within these constraints how do we answer Peter Newell's question 'What resources do people need?' (see page 108)? Perhaps we could attempt to answer this in a school like White Lion in Islington but does it entail selling people short on the qualifications that the system tells us we all need?

As well as spreading news about the success of individual projects it seems to me important to increase awareness among teachers as to the constraints on any real success and their own potential and responsibility for altering those constraints. The kind of total immersion in the inner city situation in preparing teachers seems to me the kind of experience liable to shatter traditional conceptions of professionalism and open the way for what Chelly Halsey has termed the 'new professional'. A paramount priority is to rethink our devotion to pre-service in-college theory and in-service refurbishment and move towards a kind of College of Education Without Walls where teachers are prepared not merely for analysing the niceties of nineteenth-century prose, but for meeting the realities of the inner city which are threatening the very existence of schools as we know them.

6 Solutions lie in the schools *Peter Newsam*

Although this sounds very cautious, I believe that most of what needs to be done can be carried out by educational authorities. You cannot get squarer than that. Of the developments that worry me – the lack of performance, failure of behaviour and so on within the school system – the answers lie within the educational authorities' sphere of influence. One example is theatre in education. Here are children who otherwise seem to be quite impossible to deal with, who are out of school, who are in desperate trouble with the police, but who can be seen working peacefully away at the sets down at the theatre centre. It is this variety of possibility that is open to people which is, in jargon terms, enriching the educational environment as far as they are concerned.

The feature of this kind of experimental work is that it helps us gain insights into what we might be doing within the system.

7 Back to the poverty issue – 1 *John Vaizey*

What I don't understand is why people say that you've got to have community action and all sorts of social action when quite manifestly the real problem is low wages. Why isn't there a campaign about low wages rather than a campaign about community action and community development? I think that it is because poverty has a functional role in society as we understand it. And that is probably the explanation why nothing is done about it. But I do find it most extraordinary that people don't seem to have cottoned on to the particular point of low wages.

8 Back to the poverty issue – 2 *Frank Field*

John Vaizey's contribution brings us back to what I believe is a central point in our discussion, and which is being overlooked in the scramble to propose educational reforms. We must consider whether the problems in the inner city are to be largely understood by analysing the education system, or whether the development in the inner city can only be understood by looking at the causes and extent of poverty in our society.

The official reaction to the crisis in the inner city has been spelt out by successive governments in the urban programme. The main assumption underlying those parts of the urban programme which are now in operation is that only mere pockets of poverty remain. The official view is that any crisis will be prevented from developing by 'the large and expanding programme ... in each of the major Social Services concerned'. Just how far the government's response falls short of what is required can be seen by looking at what should be the central pillar of any urban programme: namely, the guarantee of an adequate income for everyone.

This information, together with the evidence of the growing disparity between the living standards of the poorest and those enjoying an average standard of living, makes it difficult to accept the basic premise behind the urban programme – namely, that only small pockets of poverty remain. Poverty is widespread, and there is evidence to suggest that the gap between the very poor and the rest of the community is widening. Of course, the standard of living of the poorest is higher than that of the poor in pre-war Britain. But this should not blind us to the fact that we have a growing number of poor people in Britain in the 1970s, and the evidence suggests that they are disproportionately concentrated in inner city areas. The belief held by many politicians and the electorate alike, that poverty has been abolished by the welfare state, does not stand up to examination. Any programme to deal with the crisis in our inner cities must take this central fact into account.

In this final contribution Peter Brinson argues that the foundations could make a more effective effort to combat inner city poverty if they were less inclined to define quite so independently their priorities. What is suggested is a new phase in the life of British foundations. In a world of big units, often creating social problems of new dimensions, the foundations ought to collaborate on one large-scale project in the inner city. Accepting that the larger housing, education, income and employment issues will have to be left to the government, the foundations could finance all the other reforms which will be necessary for the success of the experiment. Within such a programme, foundations would be free to back those elements which come within their own terms of reference laid down by their founders.

9 Foundations and the urban crisis – a personal view *Peter Brinson*

What should foundations do about the urban crisis? By foundations I mean not just the big ones like Nuffield, Leverhulme, Wolfson, Gulbenkian – but all the fifteen hundred-odd listed in *The Directory of Grant Making Trusts*, even the very smallest. They all have something to contribute but relatively few, in fact, do contribute. Yet billions of pounds are needed to tackle the urban crisis. Only governments, it is agreed, have such money. Better, therefore, for foundations to direct their limited money where they can make more impact? It's an easy argument three times wrong which would leave foundations avoiding one of the great social issues of the day if all of them applied it. Fortunately most of the big ones do not apply it. Even so a radical reorganisation of foundations' giving is required if their grants are to make any impression on a problem this size.

During the last decade the urban crisis has come to be recognised as one of the major social problems of the day. We have seen how the deep social inequalities of our society – affecting income, housing, education and job prospects especially – can be seen in their most aggravated form within our cities. So the urban crisis becomes in turn a crisis of confidence in the processes of government and the priorities of society. Ultimately it calls in question the present social order – not without reason. The problem, therefore, cannot be ignored, so that foundations become faced with a general duty to do something about it. The human need is so enormous that, large or small, there must be something in their founding instruments which allows all foundations to take some kind of action which helps. A need so all-embracing can accept and use everything everyone can give whilst inaction, on the other hand, actually increases the need.

Apart from this general humanitarian duty there is a specific duty for very many trusts, including some of the largest. Most of them arose during the nineteenth century or in the early days of this century to alleviate particular aspects of deprivation in their time, according to priorities laid down by their founder. The greater part of this deprivation was centred in big cities. By definition, for example, the City Parochial Foundation *must* work within the Metropolitan Police District and the City of London. Hence almost the whole of this wealthy foundation's resources go to support projects which assist deprived people in inner city areas. Sometimes it gives alone; sometimes in partnership with a local authority;

sometimes with a fellow foundation. Among these the Leverhulme Trust, Nuffield Foundation, Wates Foundation, Chase Charity, Pilgrim Trust, Gulbenkian Foundation and the Joseph Rowntree Memorial Trust have shown a particular interest in inner city problems.

Since these names include some of the largest British-based foundations, why imply there is so much more to be done or even a need for reform? Because the purposes and practice of foundations were never created to cope with a problem the size of the urban crisis. The system breaks down in three ways. Its response is patchwork; it fails by and large to face a new problem with responses of a new kind; it has become – taking foundations as a whole – a muddle. Foundations in their management mostly lack incisive control, clear roles, skilled staff; rarely allocate sufficient resources to attract staff of the right quality or the research to support their decisions. Too often these decisions complement public funding with contributions of little significance. There are exceptions, especially among the more active foundations listed in *The Directory of Grant Making Trusts*, but this is the general picture from the overwhelming majority of organisations in that directory. The net result is wasteful.

It is true, nevertheless, that foundations have done good work through initiatives government will not take. This, more than anything, underlies their claim to the independence of which they are so jealous. But foundations could do better on the really major problems of deprivation if they were less inclined to define quite so independently the priorities of the moment within the interests of their founding instrument. Granted this must be observed, it does *not* follow that interpretation should be made without a careful survey of need priorities at each particular period and without reference to other trusts who have similar objectives. Very, very rarely are either of these steps taken, though sometimes reference is made to the general policies of other trusts. In the resulting patchwork some aspects of a particular problem receive more, others less attention than they would if priorities were assessed against total national need and resources after discussion between at least the major trusts working together. Such a patchwork approach is disastrous for inner city problems because it means that scarce resources cannot be directed to areas of greatest need according to a coherent plan. Nevertheless, this approach will continue as long as trusts restrict response to their own established methods, which often derive from a nineteenth-century concept of need. Patchwork response, in other words, implies a lack of new thinking in foundation grant practice.

This arises partly from a failure to identify the urban crisis early enough as something quite new in dimensions and urgency, of which Gulbenkian was as guilty as any; partly from a general feeling not confined to foundations, that the crisis is so huge and urgent one simply does not know where to begin. The latter feeling came through very strongly at the second Gulbenkian Conference.

Thus the problem of inner city need calls in question one of the basic arguments on behalf of foundations, that independence (and hence diversity of sources) inspires a creative diversity of action. This in turn throws into new perspective the third and most powerful reason why foundations should concern themselves with the urban crisis. Traditionally, foundations see themselves operating in areas where government cannot or will not move, or in areas where public spending has to be limited. The theory is that money for which government is accountable ought not to be spent too freely in areas of high risk, on experimental or minority activities. Trusts, being accountable only to themselves, assume the risk instead. They are the pioneers. Or they fill gaps in provision. Or they supplement. Or point new directions. In the section evaluating the government's response to the urban programme (see page 47) we have noted that government, local and central, has yet to will enough resources to tackle urban decay and poverty in any meaningful sense. So – almost incredibly in view of the size and urgency of the problem – there is room for foundations to fulfil their traditional role. Can this role be meaningful in so huge a field? Above all, are the assumptions behind the theory true?

The view that trusts assume risks and are more often pioneers than government is not supported today by any thorough comparison with the activities of local or central administration. The Arts Council and central government departments, for example, have initiated quite as much experiment in the arts and social welfare as any group of foundations. Foundations and trusts, in fact, are much less often the pioneers and risk-takers they claim to be. By constitution they are given to patching up the status quo. They respond but do not initiate. Response mechanisms, however, cannot generate consistent action. Hence it is inherent in the concept of most foundations to be somewhat inflexible, relatively unimaginative and rarely creative. Creative use of their potential can only come through initiatives taken after careful research having regard to other central programmes, even when acting in opposition to these programmes.

Research, then, is a fundamental need. 'It appears to us that adequate provision has not been made in the past for the organised acquisition of facts and information and for the systematic application of thought as preliminary to the settlement of policy and its subsequent administration.' This passage from the Haldane Committee's report on the machinery of government in 1918 is a sufficient comment on the methods of foundations today and a guideline for their operation in the future.

Thus the circumstances of twentieth-century need – particularly great need like inner city poverty – require of foundations not only a new kind of response – no longer passive but actively innovatory, probably collaborative, always planned on the best information available – but a new kind of staff and perhaps a new kind of foundation. Can one see such changes emerging? It will be fairest to put Gulbenkian under a microscope and let its work in inner city education throw light on the work of other foundations in the same area.

The Gulbenkian Foundation operates three programmes in the United Kingdom covering the arts, education and social welfare, all deriving from the terms of the founder's will. In 1971, when it began to take an interest in inner city education, half of all it gave away annually in UK went to the arts, totalling £250,000. The remainder was divided equally between education and social welfare amounting to £150,000 each. This had been the pattern for some years and remained so until 1975. Unlike the other two programmes, education had never had a very clear policy, so in the autumn of 1971 advice was sought from a group of educational experts. They recommended the foundation to examine four particular areas of need in the educational scene: adult education; higher education; the arts in education, including professional training for the arts; and inner city education. The first conference on *Education and the Urban Crisis* in February 1973 was a part of this examination and persuaded the Foundation of the urgency of the need. Another exploratory conference two months later on *Higher Education in the 1980s* (*Universities Quarterly*, Winter 1973) led the Foundation to defer action in this field. It took a similar decision about adult education after publication of the Russell Report. Since then it has divided its educational resources about equally between inner city education and the arts in education. Both are partners in poverty, the least subsidised, least supported areas of education needing in fact much more money than the Gulbenkian education programme could provide.

To support its educational resources, therefore, the Foundation has drawn additional resources for its two educational priorities from its arts and social welfare programmes (see *Gulbenkian 1974*,

1975 and *1976*, the annual reports of the UK and British Commonwealth Branch) recognising that inner city education is not just an
educational problem. Overlap with the other programme was
considerable and inevitable. As a result the Foundation has devoted
nearly half a million pounds to inner city problems during 1972–5,
mostly in the last three years because the programme had hardly
started in 1972. Since this is not a large sum in terms of the problem
all of it has gone to experimental projects, choice of which was
guided generally by the two Gulbenkian education conferences and
other studies. Hence grants at least were based on as thorough an
assembly of facts and advice as could be mustered.

This returns us to the laboratory role of foundations. Where
should experiments be made? If the pages of this book do nothing
more they show that there is no one solution to the urban crisis and
no one direction in which government is moving. Compare, for
example, the demands of the free schoolers with the more traditional
approach by John Vaizey and Frank Field. There are as many
solutions as there are cities, though the experience of one can help
another.

With this in mind, and against the background of advice presented
to it, the Foundation concluded there were three areas in which it
could best deploy its very limited resources: fact-gathering; action
experiments; evaluation and dissemination. In the event it concentrated on the last two, having spent a certain amount of money
already on conferences, which included fact-gathering, and noting
that other agencies had done the same. Nevertheless it is difficult
always to divorce fact-gathering from experience-gathering, particularly when the latter derives from experimental situations. The one
impinges on the other and both need a machinery for continuing analysis which does not exist at any adequate central level
to help determine priorities and deal with issues. There is, too,
the question of facts for whom? Government and local government do have departments for fact-gathering, however uncoordinated. People involved in inner city problems at grass roots
level have nothing of the kind. Nevertheless, community action
groups, street organisations, even individual families could be
much more effective in self-help and as pressure groups if they had
recourse to an independent fact-gathering agency. This is something
the Foundation is considering.

Such an attitude indicates also the general direction of the
Foundation's second area of activity, its action experiments. Apply-
ing the advice of its conferences, it has aimed here at a search for
alternatives and the development of local initiatives. Therefore its

action experiments cover three areas, all interconnected. Resource development; the encouragement of local initiatives; local stimulus and enrichment.

Under resource development come two schemes for the training of teachers for inner city areas. One is an urban studies centre in the East End of London operating under the College of St Mark and St John, Plymouth. £12,700 has been given over four years aiming to establish a centre for study and training which the college ultimately can make a permanent feature of its curriculum. A parallel scheme in the north of England gives £14,000 over three years to St John's College, York, to develop Hoyland Hall near Barnsley as an urban and community studies centre. Here too, student teachers can receive special training in problems of inner city education. In the west of the country, at Bootle in Lancashire, £7,300 over three years has been given towards the costs of a new integrated curriculum in an EPA school. Also on Merseyside, where so many inner city problems are concentrated, the Foundation is supporting two major resource experiments. One helps Liverpool University's Institute of Extension Studies to increase its programme of teaching and research in community development, citizen participation and adult education. This is primarily in the service of Merseyside's most deprived citizens but it is also experience-gathering for others working in similar situations elsewhere in Britain. The second experiment remains so far unique, a theatre-in-education team supported over three years in EPA schools in collaboration with Merseyside's Everyman Theatre and Liverpool Teachers' Centre. It applied TIE methods to a community-orientated curriculum in over 40 schools in some of the worst areas of Liverpool as a means of developing a new resource for teachers in such schools and an enlargement of the children's imaginative experience.

The Priority–Everyman Company's work, then, was in one sense resource development, in another the development of local initiatives, and in a third local enrichment. Hence it shades into the second area of foundation action-experiment because the company's programmes often dealt with local issues to encourage local initiative. Time and again both Gulbenkian conferences identified the supreme importance of self-help and community action as a principal means of tackling the urban crisis *now*: people from inner city areas themselves arousing public awareness and public resources to solve the problem. 'Intelligence enough to conceive,' as William Morris put it nearly a century ago, 'courage enough to will, power enough to compel' (*William Morris*, ed. G. D. H. Cole, Nonesuch Press, 1946, p. 661). The Foundation's own Community Work Group under Lord Boyle of Handsworth reached a similar conclusion in 1973, so this area of action-experiment is well supported by expert opinion (*Current Issues in Community Work*, Routledge and Kegan Paul, 1973).

How to achieve such action? It needs public stimulus and information combined with a selection of experiments which demonstrate alternative solutions. Granted that no one but government can fund larger experiments covering city governance, regional planning and so on, this still leaves a very wide area to foundations. First, then, alternatives demonstrating, as it were, other ways out of the crisis than those officially backed. It has not been easy to find strictly educational alternatives of this kind partly because the idea of people devising their own alternatives from their own experience is still very new; partly because one needs to find ideas which will generate a reasonable chance of future continuity once foundation support comes to an end; partly because very few alternatives in inner city education are solely educational but involve political, social and other considerations. Is it right, for example, to look for alternatives at all when resources are as scarce as we have said? Why not research the problem, decide on the solution and put all resources behind a single decision? We lack, of course, adequate research and the selected pilot experiments such research will indicate. Equally, we do not want the *ad hoc* response to uncoordinated alternatives all too often pursued under current foundation practice. Such unresearched alternatives probably lead to waste. But the decisive choice lies neither in the research nor in a particular solution resulting from research but in the philosophy guiding both. It is this alternative which needs to be tested – and can only be tested in practice.

Hence the support for Priority–Everyman in Liverpool which became a casualty of local government cuts. Its experience is enshrined in a study by John Rennie, mentioned below, as a starting point for further experiment. Meanwhile we must fight to prevent a similar fate overtaking other schemes of resource development and local enrichment.

Three of them especially are as locally based as Priority–Everyman but put philosophy to a particular test and so could modify or extend state educational practice. Two are to do with free schools. Better called community schools, these are no longer new, as White Lion Free School in Islington can testify, but they remain outside the state system, often in critical opposition to it. Barrowfield Community School in Glasgow and Balsall Heath Community School, Birmingham illustrate an important contribution their methods can make to the operation of the state education system in inner cities. Both have had different degrees of success at involving young people in an educational process which the young people had rejected in large state schools. Both schools aim at not more than about 40 pupils and both, like other community schools, have succeeded already in solving perennial problems such as truancy. Gulbenkian, therefore, agreed to contribute £11,300 over three years and £11,800 over two years respectively to see whether this kind of alternative to inner city education could not usefully provide a service for those unable to accept the state system of large schools and the curriculum, philosophy and politics implicit in such a system. The alternatives therefore test teachers as much as pupils.

Are these alternatives socially desirable? If so, to what extent should public money be devoted to them? A good case, in other words, for private subsidy preliminary to possible support from state funds.

The Foundation's response embraced three considerations. First, the growing doubts now expressed about educational justification for very large comprehensives, which is not to question comprehensives themselves. Second, the unwillingness of local government, in particular, to acknowledge that there may be other ways to solve a problem than the way worked out by city fathers and top officials. Quite apart from grassroots ideas, all too often ignored, a greater degree of experimentation by central government might be feasible – but is equally rejected. Foundation funding needs to be geared to both possibilities. Third, therefore, the Foundation accepted that the main problem of the urban crisis is not the existence of cities, or even inner city areas, but finding out how to deal with them. Hence in inner city education the problem is to discover what sort of education will meet the very special situation which inner city deprivation has created for millions of families trapped in an apparently hopeless cycle. Is the traditional emphasis on 'O' levels as the ultimate achievement really appropriate? The emphasis on 'O' levels hardly figures. If not, what other values are more appropriate? We may be able to answer these questions more clearly once the experiments in Birmingham and Glasgow begin to reach conclusions in 1976 and 1977.

The third experiment, this time within the system, is based on Sidney Stringer School and Community College, Coventry, and it is intended to add an appointment to the staff of direct value to its children. Called a Young Person Development Adviser, the appointment is a new concept to enable all children from 5 to 18 living in an area to make the best use of all the agencies available to develop their potential to the full. The arguments and reasoning behind this concept summarise many of the inner city educational problems faced by parents as well as children.

1. Many children do not have sufficient help from parents who really know how to construct a total programme of experiences to develop a child.
2. Help is only available to those who go wrong (social workers).
3. Help from teachers is concerned mainly with 'schooling' and is fragmented junior–secondary. Help stops at 16 for those who leave school for employment.
4. For many young people, the academically based school programme is inappropriate, provides little success and hence breeds alienation and discontent.
5. Many youngsters do not know what to do with their time on holidays, at weekends and in the evenings.

To face these problems the experiment argues a more flexible interpretation of the Education Act than is often brought to the Act's working. The Act specifies that people stay at school till 16, and must experience at least four hours a day of meaningful activity, directed by a teacher. It does not insist that this activity is in a school building, or is academic. A programme, designed by a teacher, agreed to by parents, which is a suitable amalgam of 'school', community and work projects, learning for leisure (music, craft, sport and outdoor pursuit, etc.) for a minimum of four hours a day would satisfy the requirements of the Act, and enable a more flexible approach to the school leaving age to be implemented. The appointment would require a teacher or social worker, sympathetic to the needs and aspirations of the young, but with a broad background and approach, appointed to the school staff but with no teaching programme. The adviser would have responsibility for the development programmes of all the children (5 to 18 years old) living within a closely defined geographical area. A case load of 120 would be appropriate. The professional works closely with the parents, and all the agencies operating in the city. Clearly, the post calls for great tact and understanding. Experience would be planned covering the whole year, and school would be seen as a part of the total experience. The Adviser might be representing parents' and pupils' views and needs to the teachers in the schools. The Service is to help the parents to develop their children to the full, and would advise and help on: schooling; non-school experiences to complement school programmes; behaviour and standards; opportunities; use of family resources; employment; relationships; resources available throughout the city.

In summary, then, the development programme should aim to overcome:

(*a*) the inflexibility of the school leaving age – so damaging for non-academic youngsters;

(*b*) the disturbing experience of transfer from junior to secondary school, and particularly from school to work;

(*c*) the alienation of many teenagers towards society fostered by inappropriate academically based school programmes.

Results should show themselves in greater development of all the potential in young people; reduced delinquency, vandalism and violence; greatly reduced truancy; better employment prospects, and employment stability; reduced pressure at school, social and probation services and so on. Thus, the idea would incorporate into the state system many elements of free school philosophy.

The idea, supported by a Foundation offer of £9,000 over three years, came from Sidney Stringer as a direct result of the Foundation's second conference and led to an appointment along the above lines in the autumn of 1975. By that time the rising unemployment of school leavers and all the other results of economic depression concentrated in inner city areas had underlined further the need for initiatives of this kind which might be alternatives or permanent additions to existing provision. The scheme will be studied in practice with more than usual attention.

Linked with this search for locally born alternatives is the provision of local stimulus, information and enrichment from which will come further local initiatives and more alternatives. Immediate inner city action is largely an attempt to raise the quality of life even within the existing decay and frustration.

This will happen most surely and successfully where people living in these areas can be faced with the problem in such a way that they understand the situation as something they themselves can act upon rather than leave improvement to the delays of local government. Experience suggests that an exceptionally fruitful way to achieve this is through the arts – not, of course, visits of the National Theatre and symphony orchestras, but the application of the arts to inner city problems through street theatre, community festivals, community arts groups, theatre-in-education and so on. The idea, of course, is not new. I quoted William Morris above and will quote George Bernard Shaw below. I might have quoted Hogarth, Goya, Dickens, Ibsen, the New Deal, Woody Guthrie and the Beatles quite apart from a tradition of strolling players and booth theatres bequeathed from classical times. What matters is that a growing number of workers in every art are now adopting this tradition to work with their public and reflect the life of that public in their art. It follows, therefore, that a particular power accrues to artists to stimulate social change and that agencies which should be concerned with social change, like foundations, cannot ignore so valuable an extra resource.

This is not to decry the value of direct community education such as the Foundation is assisting through Liverpool University. The use of the arts supplements community education and is part of it, aiming also to help people take part in the policy-making process and so strengthen democratic practice. The arts, properly used as an extra community resource, become the most immediate way to educate and stimulate through participation in words, music and movement. They can re-create local situations through local eyes to find local answers. Except that, if this is done on a big enough scale, the local answers become national answers.

There is also the theory, which the Foundation hopes to examine further, that to spend more on the arts, especially community arts and arts-in-education – in a word the development of creative leisure – is to need less for law courts and crime prevention, for combating the wear and tear on teachers and for problems which derive from parent–school misunderstandings. Certainly the Priority–Everyman experiment in Liverpool and the Granby Festival filmed by another Foundation project, the Merseyside Visual Communications Unit, both point in this direction. Local crime dropped during the Granby Festival. Through Priority–Everyman parents have been brought into closer contact with schools and children helped to understand daily events around them through a creative involvement otherwise impossible.

For all these reasons, the Foundation has attached great importance to action-experiment which encourages local initiative. We all live in communities so all can benefit from community action and participation, not least the rural communities – often as deprived as their inner city counterparts. Hence about £90,000 from the arts programme was devoted to community arts in 1974 alone, spread across Britain. Under the social welfare programme £25,000 has been given to help Ed Berman's Interaction build a new headquarters in Kentish Town, London; £5,850 in the last three years to help Interplay develop the informal education of children and young people in Leeds; £27,400 to develop Centerprise as an experimental community arts bookshop in Hackney and north-east London; £5,000 to help establish a new film and video service in education and community work on Merseyside – the Merseyside Visual Communications Unit mentioned above. And in London's East

End, £15,722 over four years to help develop a community arts team at the Albany in Deptford. Under the education programme, in addition to the resource development and education initiatives quoted above, £12,605 went to help the Hoxton-based Prodigal Trust experiment in using video as a means of extending young people's imagination and ability to communicate in four schools of London's East End. This experiment parallels the Priority–Everyman drama resources experiment in Liverpool and is itself paralleled by another East End educational experiment based on the Half Moon Theatre Company which, apart from Joan Littlewood's company, is almost the only professional theatre in the East End. Like other professional companies, it wishes to develop educational work for young audiences alongside its professional performances, but is doing this in a way designed to meet the special deprivations of inner city life. Hence the Foundation is supporting an extension of the company's youth workshops. These introduce young people to creative theatre work and so help to enrich and realise talents usually wasted in the cultural desert of an inner city. Further local action-experiments are being funded, too, in Edinburgh, Sheffield, Coventry and other cities. Nationally, embracing the whole country, the Foundation has provided £9,000 to help establish a Standing Conference of Theatre-in-Education and Young People's Theatre Groups. A majority of these companies work in inner city areas and a tremendous strengthening of their work and influence should flow from the exchange of ideas and the national voice made possible by a Standing Conference.

Three comments on these grants. First, a majority of the projects involve more than one foundation. They are not solely Gulbenkian projects. The Albany, Deptford, for example, also received grants from the City Parochial Foundation as well as statutory bodies. City Parochial helped Centerprise which raised additional funds from Chase Charity and the Sir Robert Sainsbury Charitable Fund as well as Urban Aid, the Arts Council and the local authority. Interplay in Leeds gained support from the Stanley Buxton Trust, the Joseph Rowntree Memorial Trust and the Stringer Bequest as well as the Yorkshire Arts Association, the Young Volunteer Force Foundation, the Arts Council, the Community Relations Commission and the National Playing Fields Association. The pattern is repeated time and again and is important enough to make us return below to the significance of such collaboration between foundations.

Second, even where Gulbenkian is the only foundation contributing to a project such as at Hillside High School, Bootle, or the Urban Studies Centre under the College of St Mark and St John,

Plymouth, it is usually on a condition of additional support from local sources. Often this comes from the local authority, as at Bootle, but sometimes it is from another source such as the College of St Mark and St John Foundation. In other words foundations use their money to stimulate other money, especially permanent funds for the future. Very rarely do they expect to carry the full burden themselves.

Third, none of these projects from wherever supported, be they experiments in resource development, educational alternatives or use of the arts to inform, stimulate and enrich, will have lasting value unless the results are disseminated for others to apply the lessons. Hence some provision for evaluation is usually written into each experiment. Therefore evaluation and consequent dissemination form the third important field of Gulbenkian activity and inner city affairs. John Rennie, for example, Community Education Adviser in Coventry, is evaluating the Priority–Everyman experience. And when a student drama group from University College London asked for £1,000 to take drama and play productions to inner city areas during summer 1974 the Foundation responded on condition a report was produced for publication to encourage other student drama groups to do the same. The result was Cirkusact's immensely successful *There's a Whole Fair up on the Green* published by Scanus; inspiring, one hopes, a new form of student service to the community.

But dissemination can take a number of forms. There is dissemination for relatively specialist use like this book and the reports on Priority–Everyman and Cirkusact. These aim to encourage specialist forms of action, though there is always the hope of reaching a wider public. There needs also, therefore, to be dissemination aimed specifically at the general public. Ultimately only public understanding – outrage – action will ensure that something is done on a big enough scale to right the shame of inner city neglect. The Foundation is experimenting to this end in two particular ways, both again using artists. One is indirect, placing individual artists-in-residence in the inner city. No one can tell, of course, how an individual artist will react to a new environment – and the Foundation's artist-in-schools scheme is not confined to inner cities (see *Gulbenkian 1975*, pp. 51–2. Additionally Su Braden has been commissioned to write a study of artists-in-residence relating the Foundation's work to other experience across Britain. The study will be published in 1977) – but it would be surprising if the seven artists now in inner city environments under this scheme did not react with an artist's comment on what they find, bringing to the general public and/or to people in inner city areas a new under-standing and stimulus through their artist's vision of this life. All are in residence throughout 1975–6 so that by the autumn of 1976 we should be able to see the work of Terry Atkinson, a video artist working at Sidney Stringer School, Coventry; Tony Hill, a film artist at Park House School, Sheffield; Daniel Meadows, a photo-graphic artist at Nelson and Colne College of Further Education, Lancashire; and four artists in deprived areas of London; David Cashman and Roger Fagin, two painters at St Bernard's R.C. School, Tower Hamlets; Bruce Cole, a composer at Dalston Mill Girls School, Hackney; Thomas Baptiste, a dramatist in residence at Paddington School, London. Having moved outside traditional residences at universities into more challenging social environments, the Foundation's artist-in-schools scheme looks like making as significant a contribution to the people in whose environments they are placed as the people in these environments are making to the artists, and the two together may project to the public at large.

A more direct experiment in dissemination involves the use of writers and photographers. Late in 1973 I visited a photographic exhibition on Chelsea Football Club presented in the Photographers' Gallery, Great Newport Street, WC2. A second exhibition called *Down Wapping* (see *Down Wapping* published by East End Dockland Action Group) was presented at the same time off the main gallery. This was the work of four young photographers, collectively called Exit. It brought to photographic life the dockland areas of Wapping now almost vanished. Supposing this same team were commissioned to photograph the reality of inner city life and to record in sound the voices of its people. Might not the result produce not only a book in pictures and words, but an exhibition, slides and other material to shock the general public into some sort of realisation of what it means to live in inner cities and the outrage of public indifference?

Accordingly, Exit was commissioned to produce such a book, and the result should be visible during 1976 like the results of many other foundation projects.

The people who suffer most in inner cities are young people apparently trapped in situations they can neither avoid nor counter. In the spring of 1975 two young people from Lyndhurst Youth Club, Camden Town, proposed something similar to the Exit experiment, but concentrating on young people. By using photo-graphs and the recorded comments of young people in this depressed area the club plan to show the reality of life for thousands of young people in Britain's inner cities. It will be a concentrated picture supplementing and highlighting the larger study by Exit, the one project helping the other but reflecting in particular from the inside the way housing, education and job prospect deprivation in inner cities hit young people worst of all. The Foundation supported this project, therefore, not only because it wished to emphasise the special problems of young people but because it has drawn the conclusion that within inner cities and even within areas designated for educational priority there needs to be a further priority in favour of the young. The young justify such double priority because they are both the hope and principal casualties of the urban crisis. As far as Gulbenkian is concerned the young may become *the* priority of its inner city policy.

One returns, then, to the interrelationship of the three areas in which the Foundation has sought to deploy its limited resources: fact-gathering; action experiments of various kinds; dissemination. There can be no convincing dissemination without facts and experiment, no adequate action unless based on facts, not much point in facts and action without dissemination. And since Gulbenkian joins or is joined by so many other foundations in its inner city projects it cannot be emphasised enough that this Gulbenkian pattern can be matched equally by Wates, Sainsbury and the rest, though not necessarily with the same priorities, the same deliberate planning or the same total disbursement. Therefore foundations and trusts, are, in fact, playing a considerable part already in the urban crisis. The worry is that a relatively large effort by ten or twenty foundations seems to make such little impact. Could different methods produce more impact and a greater return on the money expended? The question returns us to the larger context of foundations as a whole.

The basic problem of the inner city is acknowledged to centre on income, education, employment and housing. Housing has decayed because of a changing distribution of resources in the city away from poorer people and poorer central areas. Opinions in this book suggest that economic change over the next quarter century is likely to accentuate rather than reverse the trend. Must we then sit back and watch the change without taking action on its consequences?

Housing certainly is beyond the resources of private trusts. So are education and job prospects in their national context. These things are for government. But government, central and local, has yet to will enough resources to tackle urban decay and poverty in any meaningful way. Urban aid to London, for example, in the four years 1969–73 amounted to precisely £7 million. 'Urban aid does not make a fundamental difference', remarked the London Council of Social Service with good reason. It could have added that the lack of resources actually amounts to a national scandal. What, then, can foundations do?

We have shown, to begin with, how a variety of action embracing fact-gathering, experiment and public information lies within the capacity of a single foundation operating a coherent but individual plan deriving from the interests laid down in its founder's will. To pursue this plan two conditions had to be fulfilled. First, internally, Gulbenkian had to recognise it was not dealing exclusively with an educational problem even though educational need was the starting point. For such action as it took to be meaningful the Foundation had to draw on its resources across the board so that the operation became a combined arts–education–social welfare undertaking. Second, externally, there could have been no meaningful action in most projects without funds from other trusts. Such collaboration was *ad hoc*, trusts getting together individually without any overall plan. But are there not lessons here? If one foundation can do what, say, Gulbenkian has done, or Rowntree, or City Parochial, how much more could be achieved if all foundations worked together in a coordinated way? And by all I mean all, not just the ten or twenty already involved.

The combined annual give-away money of the twenty-odd largest trusts in the United Kingdom amounts to about £10 million. This is only a fraction of the £100 million or so which Benedict Nightingale in *Charities* estimates to be the total investment income of all the nation's charities put together. So the urban crisis poses a moral question for foundations; whether in a world of big units often creating social problems of quite new dimensions they ought not to tackle these problems by collaborating in large-scale action rather than continuing their traditional ways through small-scale independent projects. What sort of large-scale action?

Gulbenkian's internal experience points an answer. We learned we had to tackle the problem across the board. The concept of educational priority in other words is valuable but too limited. Halsey himself points out that inner city educational problems cannot be treated in isolation. What is needed is not educational priority but *social* priority involving a devotion of resources, planning, and action in meaningful amounts to designated social priority areas where can be applied also the lessons of EPAs, CDPs and urban aid programmes during the last ten years.

If government declares such a plan too expensive at the present time let it collaborate with foundations in just one area. By doing so at least it will offer hope to inner cities. In that area let it tackle the larger housing, education, income and job problems itself but leave to foundations acting in concert over say five years the wide range of related activities, experiments and services (community relations, theatre-in-education, youth work, community education and so on) which are inseparable from such an undertaking. Let government and foundations together, in other words, test the validity of an idea and the manner of its execution. So far as foundations are concerned this will entail no departure from their founders' interests. Each foundation could operate within its own sphere, but in consultation and collaboration.

So much for one possible area of government–foundation collaboration. Another purely foundation collaboration might derive from the missionary function of foundations. 'In the nineteenth century', remarks Nightingale in *Charities*, 'it might have been enough for voluntary organisations to *do*: now that the state does so much, their function is increasingly to *speak*, and to speak on behalf of those who are not getting a reasonable share of what the state has to offer.' In this sense the combined resources of even a few trusts might transform the urban crisis through a campaign of public education. The very independence of foundations fits them for this role better than a government agency.

At stake is the removal of what Stuart Hampshire called at the first conference 'the overwhelming evil'. The removal, of course, *will* happen because of 'those enthusiasts', remarked by Bernard Shaw, 'who still refuse to believe that millions of their fellow creatures must be left to sweat and suffer in hopeless toil and degradation whilst parliaments and vestries grudgingly muddle and grope towards paltry instalments of betterment' (address to the British Association, *Fabian Essays* (1931 ed.), pp. 186ff.). The duty of everyone is to hasten the day, and the function of foundations is to help encourage action in every way, including official action. We have shown what can be done and how. Foundations will be successful in a task of such immensity, not only to the extent that their help is well planned and well placed, but to the extent that it is magnified in value through collaboration. Having, one hopes, 'Intelligence enough to conceive, courage enough to will' collaboration will give them Morris's third element of action – 'power enough to compel'. Even if the compulsion looks more like inducement, power is what matters. Time is short.

List of delegates to both conferences

REX ALLEN Director of Macmillan Ltd

JOHN ANDERSON Principal, College of St Mark and St John Foundation, Plymouth

LORD ANNAN Provost, University College London

DICK ATKINSON Teacher, Balsall Heath Community School

CHRISTOPHER BAGLEY Reader in Sociology, University of Surrey

JOHN BAZALGETTE Chairman, Research Programme, Grubb Institute

JOHN BENINGTON Coventry Workshop

RHODES BOYSON MP, formerly headmaster, Highbury Grove School, Islington

PETER BRINSON Calouste Gulbenkian Foundation UK and Commonwealth Branch

JEROME BRUNER Professor of Psychology, University of Oxford

SIEGLINDE BUCKLEY Parent/Leader of children's playgroup in Birmingham

GEOFFREY CLARKSON Director, Young Volunteer Force

PETER CLYNE Assistant Education Officer, ILEA

FRANK COLES Senior Tutor, Urban Studies Centre, College of St Mark and St John

VERA COLES Community Worker, Tower Hamlets

DAVID CORKEY Ex-Albany

TOM CRITCHLEY Community Programmes Department, Home Office

PAUL CURNO Social Work Education Adviser, Central Council for Education and Training in Social Work

FIONA DUNCAN Calouste Gulbenkian Foundation UK and Commonwealth Branch

DAVID EVERSLEY Senior Research Worker, Centre for Environmental Studies

FRANK FIELD   Child Poverty Action Group and the Low Pay Unit

D. FISKE   Chief Education Officer, Manchester Education Department

A. NICHOLAS GILLETT   Lecturer in Education, University of Bristol

JOHN GREVE   Professor of Social Administration, University of Leeds

PATRICIA HAITKIN   Head of General Studies Department, South Thames College

PETER HALL   Professor of Geography, University of Reading

A. H. HALSEY   Director, Department of Social and Administrative Studies, University of Oxford

STUART HAMPSHIRE   Warden, Wadham College, Oxford

HENRY HODGE   Child Poverty Action Group/school governor

DR ROBERT HOLMAN   Childcare Community Project, Church of England Childrens Society

GEOFFREY HOLROYDE   Principal, Sidney Stringer School and Community College

BETTY HYAMS   formerly Calouste Gulbenkian Foundation UK and Commonwealth Branch

KEITH JACKSON   Institute of Extension Studies, University of Liverpool

VALERIE JENKINS   Head, Haverstock School

JANE JESSEL   Deputy Editor, *Roof*/school governor

STEPHEN JESSEL   Education Correspondent, BBC Radio, previously Education Correspondent, *The Times*

W. R. KNIGHT   Assistant Education Officer for Special Services, Yorkshire (West Riding) County Council

ALAN LITTLE   Director of Reference and Technical Services, Community Relations Commission

JOHN MACBEATH   Barrowfield Community School, Glasgow

STUART MACLURE   Editor, *Times Educational Supplement*

MARGARED MADEN   Head, Islington Green School, London

VIRGINIA MAKINS   *Times Educational Supplement*

ERIC MIDWINTER   Head of Public Affairs Unit, National Consumer Council

MICHAEL MILLER   Professor of Education and Sociology and Director of the Urban Studies Centre, New York University. Visiting Fellow at the Centre for Environmental Studies

PATRICK MILLER   Director of Social Studies, Basingstoke Sixth Form College

RICHARD MILLS   Calouste Gulbenkian Foundation UK and Commonwealth Branch

JACK MONCUR   Teacher, Ainslie Park High School, Edinburgh

JOHN MOORES   Chairman, Welfare Organisations Committee, Liverpool

LUIS GOMES MORENO   formerly Calouste Gulbenkian Foundation Lisbon

PETER NEWELL   Worker, White Lion Street free school

PETER NEWSAM   Chief Education Officer, ILEA

RAY PHILLIPS   Information/Research Officer, Newham Education Concern

REG POOLE   Chief Executive Officer, Liverpool Council of Social Service

A. W. PETERSON   formerly Permanent Head of the Home Office

BARNEY PLATTS MILLS   Governor of the British Film Institute

JIM PORTER   Principal, Bulmershe College of Education, former member of the James Committee

GEOFFREY POULTON   Director, New Communities Project, Havant

HUGH DE QUETTEVILLE   Secretary, Sainsbury Group of Trusts

JIM RADFORD   Director, Manchester Council for Voluntary Service

JOHN RENNIE   Community Education Adviser, Community Education Project, Coventry

JACK REYNARD   Home School Unit, Liverpool

JOE ROGALY   *Financial Times*

ANDREW ROWE   Home Office Voluntary Services Unit

DAVID SHAPIRO   Reader in Government at Brunel University

BRIAN SOUTHAM   formerly editor, Routledge & Kegan Paul

ANTHONY STEEN   MP, formerly director Young Volunteer Force

LORD VAIZEY   Professor of Economics, Brunel University

ROBERT WAGSTAFF   Curriculum Co-ordinator, Hillside High School, Bootle

PAULINE WARREN   Calouste Gulbenkian Foundation UK and Commonwealth Branch

MALCOLM WICKS   Home Office Urban Deprivation Unit

COLIN WILKINSON   Merseyside Visual Communications Unit

ANTHONY WILSON   Secretary, Barrow and Geraldine S. Cadbury Trust

HARRIETT WILSON   Senior Research Fellow, Warwick University, founder member and vice-chairman of Child Poverty Action Group

ARTHUR WYNN   Social researcher

MARGARET WYNN   Social researcher, author of *Fatherless Families* and *Family Policy*